About the Author

Dr. S. S. Rana; born in 1936 in village Saidpur in Haryana; B.A. (Hons.), Punjab; M.A. (Sanskrit), Ph.D, Delhi; taught at different colleges of the University; elected to the Academic Council (1975-76); Head of Sanskrit Department (1975); Principal Shivaji College (1976-88); Dean of Colleges (1988-2000); was member of (i) Board of Secondary Education), (ii) State Naming Authority, Delhi, (iii) Academic Council and Executive Council of Shri Lal Bahadur Shastri Sanskrit Vidyapeeth, (iv) Board of Governors and Board of Management of the Dev Sanskriti University, Haridwar, (v) Team for Final Review of 20-Volume Encyclopaedia of Hinduism (vi) Chancellor's Nominee in the Court of Deenbandhu Chhotu Ram University of Science and Technology, Murthal; additional charge as (i) NCC Officer in Shivaji College (1963-72), (ii) Staff Advisor, Delhi University Students' Union (1983-85), (iii) OSD (Principal) Ramjas College, Delhi (1982), (iii) OSD (Controller) Examinations, Delhi University (1985); three books and several papers published; Sanskrit Sahitya Seva Samman by the Sanskrit Sahitya Academy of NCT, Delhi (2000); Shashi Bhanu Award for Education (2012); mentored 12 M.Phil and 11 Ph.D students; visited–Bhutan, Sri Lanka, Australia, Singapore, Hungary, Japan and USA; served as Secretary (1998-2001) and Vice-President (2001-2007) of Surajmal Memorial Education Society, New Delhi.

Jāt
The Label and The People

Dr. S S Rana

Originals

Delhi

First Published 2015

ISBN 13: 978-81-8454-147-2
ISBN 10: 81-8454-147-3

Published by
Originals
A-6, Second Floor, Nimri Commercial Centre,
Ashok Vihar Phase-4, Delhi - 110 052 (India)
Tel.: +91 11 2730 2453 Fax: 011 4706 1936
website: www.LPPindia.com
e-mail: info@LPPindia.com

Printed at
IIP Printers
Delhi

PRINTED IN INDIA

Contents

Preface

The decade bisected by the culmination of the last and the inauguration of the new century landed me into an active role involving myself with the seminars on the themes of Jat history and life organized by the Research and Publication Centre of the Surajmal Memorial Education Society under the inspiration of the Late Shri Ram Niwas Mirdha. Living a retired life I found the involvement not only engaging but also challenging. Apart from giving full attention to the presentations made at the almost annual seminars I cast my net wide for accessing material on Jat history and identity. I Myself being a Sanskrit student throughout my career I do not recall having noticed the term Jat used as a caste name any where in the ancient Sanskrit literature. But when proceeding further to understand the issue I was confronted with a chorus of claims on the origin of the term 'Jat' based on the faulty interpretation of some texts of the celebrated Sanskrit grammarian, Panini of about the fifth century B.C. and some other Sanskrit text. On a deeper examination I found these claims quite unacceptable. Some of these propositions turned out to be trivial and a few quite laughable.

The outcome of my research on the subject was a comprehensive and rather longish article which I wanted to share with all those who may be interested in the issue of the identity of the term 'Jat' and how it came to be used in the sense of a caste and also how the term acquired a pejorative connotation. During the same period I also happened to contribute short (for constraints of space) essays on Jat Life and Ways for publication in the Society's Bulletin 'Suraj Sujan' and 'Jat Vshwa Gaurav'an organ of the Vishwa Jat Aryan Foundation. From the communications that I received from some readers from time to time I felt encouraged to continue the course. As an interim step I thought of publishing my research article dealing with the issue, along with some short essays at one place in book form for the benefit of those who may like to go through my submissions at leisure without losing track.

Some of the essays included in this volume might, at places, contain matters partly dealt with in others. I thought it better not to edit such spots as that would be retrospective writing. In stand alone essays the repeats did not show up. The indulgent readers would, I hope, construe accordingly.

I am fully conscious of the asymmetry of the contents of the book. But in the given circumstances I could not present it the way I had desired most.

I extend my sincere thanks to Shri S. P. Singh, President of Surajmal Memorial Education Society, New Delhi for his help and co-operation in several ways.

I would like to thank Shri J.P. Vidyalankar, the editor of 'Suraj Sujan', with whom I had the benefit of having discussions on several occasions for my firming up of interpretations of certain Sanskrit texts.

My thanks are due to Col. (retd.) O. P. Sidhu, the editor of 'Vishwa Jat Gaurav' for his eliciting from my pen some of the articles for publishing in his periodical which I have included in this volume.

I would not fail to remember here the late Dr. Vir Singh, the founder Director of the Research and Publication Centre, for his untiring zeal in enlisting the co-operation of scholars from all over India, year after year, in conducting the periodical seminars and getting the proceedings published regularly.

Last but not the least, I am thankful to Shri Pradeep Mittal for undertaking the publication of this volume and bringing it out in record time.

New Delhi, 16 August 2014 **S. S. Rana**

1

Jāt: The Label and The People

Some Insights into the Question of Origin of the Jāts and their Identity

Few questions of Indian history have elicited so varied answers, some like the opposite poles as the question of the origin and identity of the people who are called or call themselves Jāt. While many European scholars and others following them in India have tried to trace a foreign origin of the Jāts there are others, quite over whelming in number, who believe the Jāts to be the people of the Aryan stock of the Vedic India. Among adherents of the later theory there are again two schools- one holding that the Aryans themselves were the invaders ousting the earlier settlers of the Indus Valley (the Dravidians) and the other maintaining that the Aryans were the original inhabitants of the *Sapta Sindhu* region and that they, at different times of history, had been contributing to the migrations to far and near continents of the world and hence their traces to this day are found in far off regions. One thing strikingly common in the approach of almost all the scholars is their focus on the word 'Jāt'- a label and very little allowance given to the people –the content. In other words philology has all along tended to decide the issue in utter disregard of ethnology.

Further, almost all the scholars (or writers!) dealing with the question of the origin of the Jāts started with the presumption that the word Jāt was of Sanskritic origin. Phonetic similarity, however remote, became a pole star for many of them in tracing the origin of the Jāts. In offering different etymologies of the word Jāt, sound rather than sense remained their point of focus with little regard shown to the well known principle that 'sound' etymology was no sound etymology. Hence we have the theories of the Jāts being identical with the *Jartas*, Jarttikas or *Jatrikas* of the Mahabharata[1], the Shakas (the Indo Scythians)[2], the Hunas[3], the Juts of Jutland[4], the Gaete, Yuti and Yetha[5] of the Oxus region. The advocates of the Aryan origin depended largely on the language argument, which was silenced with the dictum "language is no proof of race'. Then there are some absurd theories of the origin of the Jāts, viz. from the Hair (*jatā*) of Shiva[6], the Jāthar theory of Angad Sharma[7], which does not deserve to be taken seriously for its very obnoxious and slanderous premises. Hukam Singh Pawar has put the latter theory to shreds by a detailed critique[8]. Qanungo's theory of Yadu origin[9] is equally untenable though it has many supporters as it puts reliance on Al-Biruni's description of Vāsudeva, father of Krishna, as Jāt. Thakur Deshraj[10] traces the origin of the Jaats to the Aryans of Sapta Sindhu leading us through a long discourse on the origin of the word Jāt in various similar sounding words in the old Sanskrit texts like the Mahabharata. Hukam Singh Pawar[11] delves on the question of the migrations of the Jāts to distant lands and then their subsequent return and then proceeds to derive the word Jāt from all sorts of Sanskrit words having some phonetic

---

1 Vaidya, C.V.; History of Medieval India, Vol. II, 1979, pp. 86 ff.

2 Todd, James; Annals and Antiquities of Rajasthan, Vol. I, p.85; Vol. II, pp.138, 180, 299.

3 Dahiya, B.S.; Jats: The Ancient Rulers, 1990, pp. 3, 6, 222.

4 Ibid, pp. 1, 5.

5 Advocates of the theory of Shaka origin of the Jaats (like Cunningham) cite these terms as different shades of the term Jaat.

6 Based on Devasamhita, a Sanskrit text written probably by Gorkh Sinha in early medieval period, referred to by Thakur Desh Raj in his Jat Itihas (Hindi), 1934, p. 236.

7 Based on an interpolated text in the Padmapurana. Angad Sharma's Sankrit pamphlet (Jatharotpatti, not available now) has been referred to by K.R. Qanungo in his History of Jats, 2003, p. 9.

8 Pawar, Hukam Singh, The Jats: their Origin, Antiquity and Migrations, 1993, pp.33-39 and pp. 1-30.

9 Qanungo, K.R., History of Jats, 2003, pp.10-13 ff.

10 Thakur, Desh Raj; op. cit. pp. 58-109 ff.

11 Pawar, Hukam Singh; op. cit. pp. 1-30 ff.

resemblance with it. B.S. Dahiya[12] traces the occurrence of names of modern day Jāt clans in different parts of the world especially central Asia, which he thinks was the original home of the Aryans, who migrated to the Saptsindhu region in the most ancient times. Dahiya goes as far as identifying the Jāts with the Kushānas, the Hunas and the Shakas amid many others.

All the above three scholars were Jāts. Their Jāt sensitivities some times swayed them over board in their zeal to ascribe a hoary antiquity to the Jāts. They focused on the word Jāt and tried to trace it in the ancient Indian sources. Finding no direct reference they tried to fall back upon terms having sounds similar or nearly similar to this term without reference to the historical context and ethnological connection. They do not fail to mention like many others that the word Jāt is derived from the Sanskrit root *Jata/ Jhata* s*anghāte* given by Pāṇini in his *Dhātupātha* (list of verbal stems).It is claimed that since the Jāts were republican (organized in *Saghas*) people Pāṇini's mention of the root *Jata* is with reference to the term Jāt i.e. the republics. But by this logic Jāt becomes the description of any republic-not necessarily of Jāts. In the first place Pāṇini's rules do not permit the formation jat from the root jat as the same signifies sanghata i.e. a cluster of insentient beings. Sanghata and sangha are not the same. More over we know for certain that there were numerous republics through out the Indian sub-continent with which the Jāts alone could not be connected. Further how is it that only some of the republican people of North and Northwest India are today known as Jāts. But before or during the time of Pāṇini we do not find the mention of Jāts in any reliable source of ancient literature (in Sanskrit, Pāli or Prākṛt) including inscriptions. There could not have been a complete boycott of the term Jāt for several millenniums as that would mean a complete boycott in literature of the people who mattered in the North and North-West regions of India both for their munificence and military might. B.S. Dahiya[13] and Hukam Singh Pawar[14] point out numerous references to the Jāts by their

12 Dahiya, B.S.; op. cit. pp. 6-10 ff.

13 Ibid, p.1.

14 Pawar, Hukam Singh; op. cit. p. 336.

clan names in ancient literature. But the learned scholars have failed to cite any authentic example of the reference to the same people directly by the term Jāt. Nor has either of them tried to explain why the term Jāt is missing in all such references except attributing the phenomena to a conspiracy of the Brāhmanical writers[15] which in itself appears to be a biased view. The *bias* or the *conspiracy* as they call it could not have been perpetuated so consistently through out several millenniums. And if at all there was a conspiracy how is it that the *gotra* and clan names of the same people were not missed by the same writers? And I hope it can not be their case that the ancient Indian writings came only from Brāhmanical pen. We have detailed accounts of India including the territory inhabited by the forefathers of the modern day Jāts left behind by Greek and Chinese travellers. The word Jāt is nowhere to be found in these accounts. However, indirect references are sought to be advanced in this behalf which will be examined later. Some like Grierson[16] have erroneously sought to find link of the Jāts with the terms *Jatāsur*a and *Jatādhara* mentioned in the Brihatsamhitā of Varāhamihira. Both these terms occur separately as names of two different demons in the above said text. Dahiya has also cited this reference in a bid to link the Jāt clan Jatāsarā with these two words.[17] What does Dahiya want to say? The Jatāsarā Jāts have demonstrated no signs of demonic ancestry, we believe. Apparently both the above terms appear to have hairy connection perhaps coined to underline the wild nature of the concerned characters.

In relation to the theories of foreign origin of the Jāts the following questions arise.

1. What was the original home from where the Jāts migrated to north-west India and what made them migrate to India.? And where did the Vedic literature arise?

2. What elements of their past 'foreign' identity are traceable in their life, language and culture today?

15 Dahiya, B.S.; op. cit. p. 71.
16 Quoted by Qanungo; op. cit. 2003, p. 6, note 11.
17 Dahiya, B.S.; op. cit. p. 241.

3. Who were the people displaced by the Jāts and what elements of their life language and culture are traceable in the Jāt area if assimilated by the Jāts?

4. How do we explain the consistent occurrence of the Jāt clan names in ancient Indian literature starting with the Vedas?

The answers offered in relation to the above questions by various advocates of the theory of foreign origin of the Jāts have not stood the scrutiny of many a researcher. Therefore it is not proposed here to delve on the question at length. Suffice to say with Dr. Trumpp and Reams[18] that since no incontrovertible evidence is forthcoming in favour of the foreign origin we should assume that the ancestors of the present day Jāts were indigenous people.

Nevertheless the questions of the origin and of the identity of the Jats are interlinked or rather intertwined and therefore need to be examined together.

We may now, briefly refer to the views of Hukam Singh' on the subject. Firstly Hukam Singh, citing some similarities between the life and practices of the Scythians and those of the Jāts advances the theory of Scythian origin[19] of the Jāts and gives an interesting twist to his theory by identifying the Scythians i.e. the Shakas as one of the races of the original vedic stock of Aryans of the Sapta Sindhu, thus turning full circle in his approach. Hukam Singh has listed a few similarities of customs of the Shakas and the Jāts. Thakur Deshraj had said almost the same thing more than eighty years ago.[20] Both the scholars have dexterously steered clear of the foreign origin of the Jāts via the Shaka route. But the chances of a major migration followed by another reverse migration into North-West India do not look plausible. It is not to say that migrations and reverse migrations did not take place at all. We have the cases of many people of Jāt clans like Tarars, Gathwals and Waraichs taken by invader Mahmud to Ghazni, some of whom

18 Quoted by Westphal Hellbusch, Sigrid and Westphal, Heinz; The Jat of Pakistan, 1964, p. 96.

19 Pawar, Hukam Singh; op. cit. pp. 174-213.

20 Thakur Desh Raj; op. cit. p. 67.

remigrated back to India in Rajasthan, Haryana and Uttar Pradesh escaping through the squeezing Afghan areas.[21] In this connection we may refer to the observations of German scholar couple Sigrid Hellbusch Westphal and Heinz Westphal who have aptly remarked: "*Simply by reason of their tribal name the Jāts were identified with the Scythians, Getae, the Goths and the inhabitants of Jutland- a part of Denmark. Once the identification has been made there can always be found some single parallels in customs and institutions which can be used to support the hypothesis. Starting with such assumptions, the supposed history of the Jāts, was written for a period of 2500* years."[22] It is essential, therefore, to adopt a holistic approach in tackling the question of the origin and identity of the Jāts.

Hukam Singh's imagination knows no bounds when, in an attempt to ascribe a hoary past to the Jāts (which in any case, they have), he seeks to link the term *Jāta* with the term *jātya* explained etymologically by Yāska as-*jātya-ātnāra*.[23] Hukam Singh states that *jātya* referred to here is Jāt and *ātnāra* means a nomad. The full phrase according to him refers to the Jāt nomads. To bolster his stand in utter disregard of the structure and semantics of Sanskrit language, he gives a fanciful meaning of *ātnāra* i.e. one who has *ātana* (coarse hardening of the skin) on the joints of he toes (should it not be on the pads of the palms?). Outdoing Hukam Singh in making fanciful suggestions, Dahiya alters the text itself from *ātnāra* to *jātanāra*.[24] It is highly misleading if not done inadvertently. But we know that the people of the Vedic Aryan stock were sedentary people settled in villages, tilling their lands (which were quite fertile) and did not have the need to move from place to place as nomads in search of their livelihood. Kautilya[25] prescribes the settlement pattern of the people in villages having a minimum of one hundred families and a maximum of five hundred

21 Westphal Hellbusch, Sigrid and Westphal, Heinz; Zur Geschichte und Kultur der Jat, Berlin, 1968, p. 113.

22 Westphal Hellbusch, Sigrid and Westphal, Heinz; The Jat of Pakistan, 1964, p. 95.

23 Pawar, Hukam Singh; op. cit. p. 153.

24 Dahiya, B.S; op. cit. p. 22.

25 Arthashastra, 2.1.2.

families, corroborating the existence of a stable agricultural economy in India in very early times. Kautilya must have had in view also the tract of Saptasindhu when he wrote about the above subject.

Hukam Singh continues to jump from one stride to another linking the word Jāt with any thing sounding howsoever remotely similar to it. He devotes great deal of effort linking the Jāts to the republican confederacy through the route of Pāṇini who lists the verbal stem *jata/jhata* meaning a cluster. Hukam Singh does not wait for a moment before concluding, as many others have done earlier, to read the meaning of a political entity (confederacy-*sangha*) in the term *sanghāta* rather than a simple meaning of cluster or a thicket—a meaning which is well indicated by the term *jātya*–a mendicant with long locks of hair referred to by Yaska.[26] Another version of the word is *jatila* derived from the root *Jat*, used by Kautilya[27] in the sense of a person having matted hair. The word *Jatā* in the sense of matted hair occurs with fair amount of frequency in the Sanskrit literature. It is interesting to note how Hukam Singh is going in rounds of now take, now leave the particular meanings of words as it suits his line of argument. He reaches the peak of his fancy when he hints at the *jatā pātha* of the Rigveda to do something with the Jāts who he thinks were the redactors of the Rigveda Samhitā. Any one, even remotely conversant with the system of presentation of the Rigvedic readings in *Jatā* (interlocked fashion) form, would be amused at the insinuation not withstanding Hukam Singh's perambulatory marshalling of a host of material in support of his line of argument. If that was not enough, then he has several other alternative suggestions to hammer his point that the word Jāt occurs in ancient Indian texts (no matter in what *avatāra*). So we find him saying that the term Jāt has its origin in *Jata*, the name of a commander of the forces of Kārttikeya, the mythical son of the mythological god, Shiva[28]. No holds are barred for Hukam Singh when he derives the word from Yayāti (again a mythical character)

26 Nirukta, I.14.

27 Arthashastra, 1.11.13,14; 1.13.15; 7.17.5.

28 Pawar, Hukam Singh; op. cit. p. 342.

via < *Yayāta* < *Yajāta* <*Jajāta* < Jāt[29]. His marshalling of words like *Jāta* and *Sujāta* is part of the same exercise. This is not serious stuff for examination of an important ethnological and historical issue. It is clear that Hukam Singh himself is not clear as to what route to follow to get at the root of the term Jāt.

Thakur Deshraj also falls prey to a similar line of investigation. His attempt to trace the origin of the word Jāt, first directly to the Pāṇinian root *Jata/Jhata sanghāte* and then resorting to mythology to link the term to another original *Jnāti* With soft 't', which, traveling through *Jnātā* and *Jāta* finally becomes Jāt.[30]

Equally queer is the approach of B.S. Dahiya[31] who prefers to derive the term Jāt from Yodhā/Jodhā and paints the whole of Indian history with the Jāt brush. He has made a painstaking study of the clan names of the so called Jāts and finds them any where and any time. He has commandeered enormous amount of material starting from the Rigveda where he traces names of many Jāt clans. But his approach is unilinear in which he bends many a principle of interpretation and language comprehension. He dabbles into interpretation of Sanskrit texts without having proper access to the correct tools. A glaring example is his incorrectly reading *varkan* (=Virk) in place of *avaskanna* in the Mandasor Pillar Inscription of Yasodharman[32] simply to justify his presumption that Yasodharman was a Jāt (of Virk clan). He also believes that the example given by grammarian Chandragomin *ajayaj-jarto Hunan* refers to Yasodharman[33]. In this way Dahiya appears to suggest that the word Jāt is derived from *Jarta* without considering whatever happened to his stand that the word is derived from Yodhā/Jodhā. Dahiya cites Yasodharman's clan name *Aulikara* to ascribe him a Jāt identity of an Aulakh.[34] In the same strain he identifies the Mor clan of the Jāts with the Mauryas who, he says, were all Jāts. He

29 Ibid, p. 186.
30 Thakur, Desh Raj; op. cit. pp. 106-07, 181.
31 Dahiya, B.S.; op. cit. p. 6.
32 Line 4 of Mandasor Pillar Inscription of Yashodharman, in Sircar, D.C. Select Inscriptions,Vol. I, pp. 418 ff.
33 Dahiya, B.S.; op. cit. p. 22.
34 Ibid, pp. 22, 210.

forgets that Mor or Maurya is a clan name not exclusively of the Jāts. His treatment of the word *Maud*[35] linking it with Maurya is to say the least amusing. This word is clearly derived from *Mugad*< *Muguda*< *Mukuta* (Sanskrit). Similarly Dahiya has claimed that the kings of the Gupta dynasty were Jāts.[36] It is not that he is the pioneer in this approach. Earlier K.P. Jayaswal (on the basis of a doubtful text–*Ārya-Manjushri-Molakalpa*) and Dasaratha Sharma (on the basis of similarity of the name Dhārana of a Jāt clan of Rajasthan) had separately claimed that the Guptas were Jāts. That apart, it is not understood how Dahiya insists that 'Gupta' was not a family name and that it was coincidentally a part of the personal names of some of the kings of the dynasty.[37]

Dahiya perhaps failed to notice the fact stated in many of the inscriptions of the family and their feudatories that the Guptas were known as a dynasty of that name and that an era had been founded in the name of the dynasty. The Udayagiri Cave Inscription of Kumaragupta-I[38] in line 1 refers to the Gupta family and in line 2 to the Gupta year 106. The Girnar Rock Inscription of Skandagupta mentions the year136 of the Gupta era in line 15 and similarly the year 137 in line 18 and again the year 138 of the Gupta era in line 27. The term Goptā which Dahiya associates with the Gupta kings is in fact used for feudatories in the same inscription in line 6. The Kahaun Pillar Inscription of Skandaguta in line 2 refers to him as one born in the Gupta Family. Again Skandagupta is described as a unique hero born in the Gupta family in line 7 of his Bhitari Pillar Inscription. The Khoh copper Plate Inscription of Mahāraja Hastin of the Parivrājaka family, a feudatory refers to the Gupta dynasty and the year 163 of the Gupta era in line 1. Another inscription of Mahāraj Sankshobha from the same place in a similar fashion refers to the Gupta family and the year 203 in the Gupta era in line 1. This should dispel all doubt created by Dahiya's stipulation regarding the dynastic status of the Guptas.

35 Ibid, p. 138.

36 Ibid, pp. 177-200 ff.

37 Ibid, p. 175.

38 For text of the inscriptions referred here and subsequently see Sircar, D.C.; Select Inscriptions,Vol. I.

It appears that Dahiya read a narrow meaning of the Vaish community of the modern times in the term 'Gupta'. If he had gone a little deeper into the dynamics of the emerging of clan names he would not have to go into unwarranted formulations. Shriram Goel was not deterred by the term Gupta while holding the family as Brahmanas[39]. It is a different matter to examine whether the Guptas can be identified as Jāts solely on the basis of similarity of their clan name Dhārana or on the basis of a doubtful text. It is well known that many clan names are common to several communities and quite different identities (castes). More clinching evidence is required to reach a definite conclusion. The antiquity and import of the term Jāt itself is under discussion for the present. However, there is no difficulty in conceding that the Guptas belonged to the Aryan clan of Dhārana. But surely Dahiya lands himself in a rap when he identifies the Hunas and the Guptas together as Jāts, particularly when they were contending contemporaries. His sense on the Bhitari Pillar Inscription of Skanda Gupta is hardly convincing based as it is on faulty representation of the Sanskrit text.[40]

Dahiya has also tried to stamp a Jāt identity on Harshawardhana of the Pushyabhuti dynasty by enlisting far fetched evidence. He quotes Hiuen Tsang in part when Harsha is to be ascribed the Bais (Bains) gotra but later conveniently gives a wrong twist to the categorical statement of Hiuen Tsang that Harshawardhana was a Rajputra (Rajput) of Bais Gotra.[41] His equating of Bais with Vaishya is without any basis. More amusing is his idea that in the present context the term Vaishya denotes merely the profession of agriculture of the Vaishya varna and not the *Vaishya* caste of today. How can he hold Harsha as a Rajput and a Vaishya at the same time (p.207)? Interestingly Dahiya tries to connect Harshawardhana with the Aulikaras, the Bains, the Vrikas or Virks at one and the same time.[42] It only shows that he is determined to prove by any

39 Goel, Shri Ram, History of the Imperial Guptas.

40 Dahiya, B.S.; op. cit. p. 7.

41 The Life of Hiuen Tsang by the Shaman Hwui Li, 1911, reprint, 2001, p. 83.

42 Dahiya, B.S.; op. cit. pp. 201-225.

means that Harshawardhana was a Jāt. However we have no problem in believing Harsha to be from a common stock which later yielded the two separate labels of Jaat and Rajput arising out of the Arab giving (or calling?) names in respect of their eastern rivals.

Similarly untenable is the position of the so called Sanskritic interpreters of the term Jāt. They would on the one hand, instantly connect the terms *jartta* of fourth /fifth century Sanskrit grammarian Chandragomin (vide his example *ajayat jartto hunan* to illustrate recent past) and *Jarttika* of the Mahabharata with Jāt of the later times, paying little heed to the remoteness of time (at least 1500 tears) between the two references and on the other hand visit Pāṇini for a reference to the Jāts via his listing of the root *Jata/ Jhata sanghāte* reading in it a meaning of a *sangha* (confederation) instead of a *sanghāta* (cluster). Pāṇini (5th century B.C.) happens to belong to the period between the time of the Mahabharata (not later than 1000 B.C.) and the time of Chandragomin (5th century A.D.). If *jartta* or *Jarttika* was the original term as found in the Mahabharata how did it get transformed into *Jata* in Pāṇini and then how it again changed into *Jartta* (in Chandragomin's time) and later yet again into the form *Jāta* is beyond comprehension. We can not take liberty in tracing the history of words throwing to winds all norms of scientific linguistic inquiry. The only conclusion one can draw in view of the above is that the terms *jartta, Jarttika* and *Jāta* are different from each other and stand for different entities. In fact the attempts to understand the identity of the Jāts solely through the route of the linguistic nuances regarding the term Jāt taking it to be of Sanskritic origin have landed us in a quagmire of confusion leading to serious misinterpretation of the identity of the Jāts.

In the array of surmises of presumptions about the origin of the word Jāt yet another contribution is from late Dr. Girish Chandra Dwivedi who had done seminal research on the role of the Jāts in the Mughal empire. According to Hukam Singh[43], Dwivedi[44] opines that when the existence and independence of republican

43 Pawar, Hukam Singh; op. cit. p. 153.

44 Journal of Indian History, Vol. XLVIII, pt. 2,1970, pp. 382 ff.

tribes of the Punjab and Sindh were threatened after 4th century B.C. by invaders from the west and the imperialistic onslaughts emanating from the east, these tribes, in order to protect their life, property and prestige, formed a union or federation and gave it an appropriate name i.e. Jāt, acceptable to all the federating units instead of adopting for the union the name of a particular tribe, however powerful it was, for the sake of avoiding the possibility of arousing jealousy or rivalry among them. Perhaps Dwivedi assumes that the word Jāt existed in Sanskrit language before the time of Pāṇini. Hukam Singh gives the impression that Pāṇini listed the word *Jāta* and gave its etymology. The truth is that Pāṇini merely listed the root *Jata/Jhata* in the sense of *sanghāta* (cluster or thicket) derivatives of which like *Jatā*, *jatila* and *Jātya* are found used in Sanskrit works. Manu Smriti (II.219), for example gives three types of students in a convent viz. *mundi* (those with their head clean shaved), *jatila* (those who kept their hair uncut and *shikhajata* (those who shaved their head leaving a tuft at the top. The above words are no doubt derivatives of the root *jata/jhata*. But the word Jāta per say does not occur in any Sanskrit work of antiquity. Therefore a fresh approach is necessary for tracing the history and true import of the term.

It would be useful for our enquiry to first concentrate on the known and then proceed to the domain of the unknown to understand the true identity of the Jāts. We should take a serious note of the total absence of the use of the term Jat in relation to a community in the entire Indo Aryan literature. But it should not be forgotten that the names of many Jāt clans are fairly referred to in the ancient Sanskrit works including those on grammar and other compendiums and inscriptions. The absence of reference to the term Jāt on the one hand and a fair amount of references to the ancient clans of the Jāts gives rise to the question whether the so called Jāts of later days were at all known by the term Jāt and was it not enough to be known by their respective clan names like *Yaudheyas, Ārjunāyanas, Mattamayūrakas, Bahudhānyakas, Matsaras, Kharaparikas, Kākas, Shivis, Shivaskandas, Mālavas* etc. in Sanskrit inscriptions, especially the Allahabad Pillar Inscription of Samudragupta) of a fair antiquity (4th century A.D.)

and other literature. Kautilya also mentions Sanghas like *vārta-shāstropajīvī* living by an economic vocation and the profession of arms.[45] The Greeks were conversant with several republican peoples from whom the modern day *Jāts* derive their clan names. Foreign travellers like Megasthenes (302 B.C.), Fa-Hian (401-410 A.D.) and Hieuan-Tsang (630-643 A.D.) who visited India at different points of history have left eloquent accounts of the country and its people. The word Jāt for a community is nowhere traceable in these accounts. It is however, significant that the Arab geographer Al-Biruni (meaning, the teacher and whose real name was Abu-Rehan Muhammad) who had accompanied Mahmud Ghaznavi during the latter's campaigns and who lived in Punjab for several years mentions the Jāts in his book Tahkik-e-Hind. The reference by the Arab scholar is to be marked: "Krishna was born of Kansa's sister married with Vāsudeva, a cattle rearing Jat of the shudra class."[46] Obviously Al-Biruni was using the familiar 'Arab term 'Jat' with its derogatory and contemptuous meaning for the cattle owning/rearing community of the Yādavas. No Indian informant could have given such a description of the family of Krishna in the 12th century A.D. for the benefit of Al-Biruni. It is only the Arabs and (perhaps through them the Persians who have used the familiar term Jat for their Indian neighbours for the first time and that too for people who were strangers to them and were not held in esteem.

It may be worthwhile to focus our attention on the usage of the term jat in the western region to understand its true meaning and the circumstances of its link with a class of people concentrated in a contiguous and well demarcated area of North and North west India. According to Westphal Djat. Zutt or Dyat was the name given by the Arabs to the middle Indo Aryans of the Punjab and Sindh region and is of post Sanskritic origin[47]. Even if we insist that Jāt were a caste from the very early times it is not likely that the Arabs were conversant with the finer details of the caste/

45 Arthashastra, 11.1.

46 Schau, E.C.; Al-Biruni's India, Vol. I, p. 401.

47 Westphal Hellbusch, Sigrid and Westphal, Heinz; The Jat of Pakistan, 1964, pp. 47-48.

varna system of Hindustan or the inhabitants of the tract which they called Hind. Certainly the term was used as a pejorative for the collective population of this area. It is significant to note with Westphal that in the Arabic language *Djat* and *Zutt* were written as one compound word *Djat-Zutt* to represent them as one and the same people.[48] Westphal however, missed to grasp the reason behind the compound of two units *Djat-Zutt.* Let us elaborate. We know that in western dialects of the later Indo Aryan language there is a tendency to use a term with its distorted meaningless rhyming sound in the sense of belittlement e.g. *roti-voti/shoti, chhotā-motā, kām-vām* etc. So the use of the term *Djat* as a compound *Djat-Zutt* is in the sense of belittlement or censure or contempt which the people from Sindh and Punjab region (and also beyond) earned from the unfriendly people living to their west. Westphals, however, refer to Risley's observation (in People of India, p. 309) *that the Jats are called Hindki with a touch of belittlement by the Pathans*.[49] The same authors cite also the Baluchistan Gazetteer which informs that a distinction exists between the Jāts themselves.[50] The term Jat/*Jatt* or *Zutt* therefore, has its origination in the Arabic language carrying a derogatory sense or that of belittlement. Westphals also quote observations of Major Wace:

"The real Jāt clans of the Rawalpindi division have a prejudice against the term Jat because it is usually applied to the camel-drivers, and to the graziers of the bar, whom they look down upon as low fellows. But there is, I think, no doubt that the principal agricultural tribes whom we can not class as Rajputs are really of the same race as the Jat of the Lower Panjab (Salt-Range-tract.)"[51]

Herein lies the clue for reaching the probable time when the term Jat could have been used by the Arabs for the cultivator Jāt in addition to the nomadic Jat. Perhaps the agriculturist clans of

48 Ibid, p. 48.
49 Ibid, p. 48.
50 Ibid, p. 48.
51 Westphal Hellbusch, Sigrid und Westphal, Heinz; Zur Geschichte und Kultur der Jat, Berlin,1968, p. 70.

the Rawalpindi division had realized what the term Jat stood for, hence their dislike for the same being used for them. But how its use persisted is a different story.

In a similar way the remarks of Ali Sher Ali Ansari are appropriately noted by Westphals.[52]

"The expression Jat-Bloch means 'camel-driving Baloch'. In Mir Chakar's time a number of low-caste balochis were employed in loading, leading and grazing his trains and flocks of camels, and those Balochis and their descendants were called 'Jat-Baloch'."

The following observations of Ibbetson are significant in the context of the origin and locale of the word Jāt:

"Between the Sulaimans and the great sandy deserts of Bahawalpur and the Sindh-Sagar Doab the dominant race is Baloch. Descending from the hills this Iranian people overcame a miscellaneous collection of tribes which, still forming a very large proportion of the population, have been included by their conquerors under the semi-contemptuous term of Jat–here an occupational as much as an ethnological designation–till they have themselves almost forgotten their original race."[53]

Westphals refer to Woolner's comment on how *the use of the common term Zatt or Zutt for gypsies might have been responsible for connecting the* Jats *with the Gypsies.* Further, Woolner is stated to have mentioned that *in modern Arabic this use is still found in Damascus.*[54]

Elsewhere[55] they record: *Most Baloch do not acknowledge them (Jats) as their own tribesmen, and in the extreme they will give the word Jat the meaning of a "stranger"and then use it to designate a man even otherwise known to be, let us say, Arain.*

52 Westphal Heilbusch, Sigrid and Westphal, Heinz; The Jat of Pakistan, p. 17-18ff.

53 Glossary of Tribes and Castes in North West Frontier and the Punjab, compiled by H.A. Rose, p. 17.

54 Westphal Hellbusch, Sigrid and Westphal, Heinz; Zur Geschichte und Kultur der Jat, Berlin, 1968, p. 12, fn.

55 Westphal Hellbusch, Sigrid and Westphal, Heinz; The Jat of Pakistan, 1964, p. 49.

Then there are (i) camel-rearing nomads who are Jat by caste and (ii) camel breeders/camel-drivers hired for work who are Jat by profession. Both these types bear hardly features that can connect them ethnically with the Jāts proper of India of the not so distant past, known by their clan names. Superimposition of the collective name Jāt on the people of common stock of the various Aryan clans therefore, can be ascribed to the Arabs and together with them or following them to their neighbours, the Persians. It may not be out of place to mention that the terms Jāt, Hind, Hindu, Hindustan and *Hindki* (a name of their dialect ultimately to be called Hindi) have the Arabs as authors. All these terms do not carry flattering connotations in the Arabic, Persian and Pakhtoon world even today.

The Arab conquest of Sindh gave the Arabs a sort of license to continue to so use the term (Jāt) for all subjugated people of the east who were taken to be of low social rank. Several centuries of Muslim rule followed by British rule hardly gave the hitherto called Hindustanis or Hindus an occasion to sit back and realize its intended meaning, particularly when the term (Jāt) was not an indigenous one. Digressing a little we may mention here that the area of the prevalence of the Jāts roughly corresponds to the tract described by the Arabs as Hindustan or Hind. Herbert Risley has identified and plotted on the map of India the same tract as the area of settlement of the people of Indo Aryan stock.[56] It has been known as such for several centuries till the twentieth century when an extended meaning was given to it to denote the whole territory of undivided India. The Mughals, the British and also Indian writers used the word in the sense of a limited territory. G. S. Ghurye has described Hindustan as a province of India.[57] Father Wendell a contemporary of the Jat rulers of Bharatpur used the word in the same sense in his memoirs about the rise of Jāt power in Hindustan.[58] The author of Majmul Twarikh says that *by*

56 Risley, Herbert; The People of India (map appended at the end of the book).

57 Ghurye; Caste and Race in India, 1988, p. 241.

58 Wendel's Memoirs on the Origin, Growth and Present State of Jat Power in Hindustan (1768), Edited by Jean Deloche,1991.

the Arabs all Hindus are called Jats.[59] It is important to note that before the partition all Muslims of Sindh were called Jāts. But after the partition, with Islam becoming the State religion in Pakistan the word Jāt is no more used in that sense.[60] The Question is, why? Perhaps the answer lies in the awareness among the Muslims of Sindh of the derogatory meaning of the term Jāt (and let us add also the term Hindu) prevalent in Pakistan and further west in the Arabian cultures. The religious identity as Muslims pushed the caste identity to the background. This also explains why groups like the Rajputs, Gujars and Ahirs initially belonging to the same common stock as the Jāts in awareness of the pejorative sense of the term Jāt opted for better labels having branched out through separate identities evolved with the setting up of principalities of the monarchical type.

The westerly people looking down upon the easterly people, is well noted phenomenon in Indian history. Nirad C. Chaudhary has developed it as a serious theme in his book '*Continent of Circe*' Where he has shown how the westerly people continue to have a dim view of the people relatively to their east in a chain reaction as in the manner of passing the buck (of low esteem). Haven't we seen the print and electronic media in our times referring to Chaudhary Charan Singh as the Jāt-Leader and not as leader of the Jāts or simply national leader. The same has been the treatment meted out to other prominent leaders from among the Jāts. The Jāt identity in these cases is highlighted to belittle the stature of the leader concerned in the belief that all non Jāts (ho are in overwhelming majority in our country) would relish it. We can't fail to notice the western Indians describing the easterners as *purabias* in the sense of belittlement. The same is true of the derivatives of the term Jat viz. *Jatkā* (gaudy/ not fine) colour, *Jatki* (rustic) dialect, *Jātu Boli* (rustic speech), *Jāttu khānā* (coarse meal) It therefore is quite plausible that the term Jāt in origin is an Arabic term denoting denigration or belittlement used by the Arabs for the simple and

59 Glossary of Tribes and Castes in North West Frontier and the Punjab, compiled by H.A. Rose, p. 358, fn.

60 Westphal Hellbusch, Sigrid and Westphal, Heinz; The Jat of Pakistan, p. 48.

rustic people from the North-west of India with whom the former came into contact in adversary relationship or otherwise. Thus a collective term originally used in relation to people in general belonging to the west and north west region of India, called by the Arabs as Hind or Hindustan came to be used for the main stock without reference to their specific (and subordinate) identities with which the Arabs and others in the west were perhaps not conversant. Sub-groups of communities branching off from the main stock and adopting non agricultural vocations came to be known by the new labels largely corresponding to their respective vocations for the simple purpose of describing their specific identities. With the domination of large tracts of the North and North West by the Arabs first and the other Islamic hoards later, the Jāt identity of the main stock Aryans of the north and north-west India earlier referred to by their clan names came to be described by the term Jāt. Though from a distance all members of the tract or the main stock were labelled as Jāts (this is the case even today in the eyes of undiscerning outsiders). It continued throughout the periods of foreign domination. However, in the eyes of insiders the smaller vocation wise identities had come to stabilize and came into use leaving the main set to be known by the superimposed identity of Jāt. The pressing needs of the fast emerging caste system hastened this process. Thus Jāt came to stay as a caste as every other group acquired one each for itself on the basis of vocation/ occupation (largely) or any other significant identity. Reference to the ethnological connections in the form of clan names remained a matter to come into reckoning only at the time of contracting marriages in a system of exogamy of sept (gotra) and endogamy of caste or in the organization of the Panchayats for sorting out social and several legal tussles and also for handling serious political issues affecting the lives of the people. The rise of mighty kingdoms and empires like that of the Kushānas, the Mauryas, the Guptas, the Pushyabhutis etc covering the Jāt areas daunted and pushed to the background their republican spirit. And it would not be out of place to suggest that at the fore front of the new system were many of the republican leaders of the yesteryears like the

Kurus, the Panchalas etc referred to by Kautilya.[61] The formation of the Rajput, Gurjar Abhir principalities can be cited as examples of this phenomenon which can be noticed on the eve of the Arab conquest of North-West India and during the period that followed. The commonality of many clan names (like Gehlot, Dahima, Pawar, Mor, Solanki, Yadava, Tanwar, Chauhan etc.) among these communities and the Jāts goes to indicate a common stock of all of them at some stage in the past. Herbert Risley has rightly summed up when he says that *one and the same tribe is often known as Rajput wherever it has, and Jat where it has not, risen to political importance.*[62] The different clans which did not believe in the institution of kingship and had no interest in pursuing state formation goals withdrew into isolation, regulating their social life according to their own republican traditions. Political aspirations took a back seat. The efficient and successful working of the *Khap* and *Sarva Khap* Panchayat system in vogue for several centuries in the Jāt region served as a consolation to the Jāts, who in any case did not favour a monarchic system. Dasharatha Sharma, writing on the Chauhanas makes a significant observation that "*it is not unlikely that many of the early republican people might have contributed to the formation of the present Jat caste, some becoming Rajputs and the others remaining Jat caste, according to their circumstances and predilections.*"[63] This observation can be improved upon with the proviso that the republican people referred to here them selves had no contribution to make in getting the new label (Jāt). In fact they were oblivious of its true meaning. G.S. Ghurye[64] has drawn our attention to Oscar Lewi's reference to a tradition in village Rani Khera near Delhi according to which the Bisi (a group of twenty villages) of the Dabas *gotra* are the descendants of the great grand son of the famous ruler Prithviraj, who came to live in village Rampur (near Lawrence Road New Delhi) in about 1200 A.D. Much earlier than Dasharatha Sharma, Risley, in the beginning of the last century, had made a penetrating observation: " ...*Gujars, Jats.....represent tribes which have been*

61 Arthashastra, 11.1.

62 Risley, Herbert; The People of India, p. 416.

63 Sharma, Dasharatha; Early Chauhan Dynasties, 1975, p. 280.

64 Ghurye; Caste and Race in India, 1988, p. 233.

transformed into castes at a comparatively recent date and retain some traces of the tribal stage of development".[65] Both, Risley and Dasharatha Sharma independently had a common hunch which they could not spell out with clarity as they had not explored the Arab track to trace the origin of the term Jāt.

We also need to address the question whether the terms Jāt (with hard 't') and Jat (with soft 't') represent one and the same people. Throughout the Arabic and Persian sources the people referred to by the term Jat (with short 'a' and soft 't') are the ones who best represent the lowly and humble herdsmen or graziers except with the rider that they also worked as mercenaries and guides and helpers of the invaders in times of war. And one can suggest that these functions were imposed on them under duress. Perhaps these people were first called Jats by the Arabs and latter by extension all similar looking nomads and cultivators were given the same name. Westphals[66] report an opinion in Punjab and Sindh (Pakistan) that Jat and Jāt were different, the Jāt having been cultivators par excellence for many centuries....whereas the Jats were poor nomadic people. They further quote the *Gazetteer of Punjab,* Provincial volume, Calcutta,1888-89, p.17 where it was stated that "*the Baloch and Pathan contemptuously called all people not belonging to their own tribes Jat without any regard to caste or* occupation".[67] On the other hand the Jāts (with long 'a' and hard 't' were sedentary agriculturists and husbandmen of the Hind/Hindustan roughly corresponding to the Jāt tract. Perhaps the two versions of the word Jāt represented the finer distinction between the nomads and the cultivators. But as far as the Arabs were concerned this distinction was not material. It is not to suggest that the Jāts had no nomadic characteristic. In fact cattle-rearing was an integral though secondary part of the cultivator's life. It may be surmised that *Jat* gave rise to the term *Jatt* from which the term Jāt was differentiated to denote a martial and land owning cultivator. As they say there is no Jāt

65 Risley, Herbert; op. cit. p. 126.

66 Westphal Hellbusch, Sigrid and Westphal, Heinz; The Jat of Pakistan, p. 47.

67 Ibid, p. 48.

who does not hold land. It is also however, true that all of those who hold land are not Jāts. One can venture to suggest that it were the latter who were responsible for the sublimation of the meaning of the term Jāt to a considerable extent by owning it and also flaunting it with pride as it stabilized to denote a particular class/caste of people with old roots and traditions embedded in the Vedic culture. In modern times their entry into the portals of education and access to the tools of political power has bolstered their tryst to regain the glory that once upon a time was theirs', the new label notwithstanding.

In course of time the derogatory meaning got considerably sublimated by innovations in pronunciation and emphasis. Thus we have the term Jāt as a polished version of *Jatt, a* term which differentiated the cultivator Jāt from the nomad Jat Since the derogatory meaning prevailed only in the west the eastern version Jāt alone survived eastwards from Punjab though not without carrying some shades of the derogatory meaning once attached to it. The label Jāt, though initially indicating slight, later came handy in serving as a common collective term for the many separate clans having their own separate identities especially when the Arabic connotation remained unknown to most in India. With the growth of the caste system into a rigid one the Jāts were left with the main stock identity, others being identified with the specialized caste/ occupational sub identities. The word Jāt, whatever the history of its use, has come to stay cementing a common identity of a vast section of the people of the North and North-west India. Further, the romanticizing of the Jāts by the British writers for the reason of the former having proved crucially helpful to the Empire in several wars rubbed off many layers of roughness and denigration associated with the term. Their contribution in the development of new India did not go unrecognised. As harbingers of the green revolution when it was most needed they won accolades of all countrymen. The dish was delectable, and so the Jāts have been relishing it for centuries. The modern day Jāts are the proud inheritors of their old clan names, but it would not be correct to impose the later day label 'Jāt' on them retrospectively during the period they were not known by it.

The sum total of our submission is that we need not cling to the couple of words of ancient Sanskrit language with the misconception that they represent various shades of the term Jāt in a bid to prove the antiquity and Sanskritic and Vedic connection of the Jāts. That is amply proved by philological, ethnological and anthropological evidence in ample measure marshalled by a good number of scholars. However, it may also be admitted that like may other communities the Jāts have had some amount of mixed blood for the reason of their progressive and pragmatic view of things including marriage. The Jāt clan (*gotra*) system developed in accordance with the Dharmaśāstric traditions (Appendix-1) and combined with Sanskritic nomenclatures of their intertwined familial relationships (Appendix-2), their flora and fauna (Appendix-3), their food and drinks (Appendix-4), their clothes and ornaments (Appendix-5) and their Sanskritic numerals clearly point to their being the descendants of the Vedic Aryans. However, it is important to drive attention to some core features of the Jāt life which indicate that they cannot be any thing but the indigenous Aryans of Vedic-Sanskṛtic culture. In spite of the general impression of their indifferent and unorthodox approach to Hindu religion the Jāts have demonstrated the strictest adherence to its basic tenets. It is another matter that they did not believe in the indispensability of priests and rigidity of rituals. The exogamy of gotra for four generations on the side of both male and female in contracting marriages leaves behind many zealous practitioners in espousing the Hindu traditions. The Jāts scrupulously follow the Vedic procedure laid down for Hindu marriage. They faithfully observe *Śrāddha* and offer oblations to their ancestors as prescribed in the Hindu scriptures. They start all important endeavours with a prayer to Rāma, representing God and are generally prone to be followers of the Aryasamaj. The mere fact that the label Jāt is of foreign (Arabic) origin does not go to establish the foreign identity of the Jāts. They are the ancient indigenous Aryan people carrying on with their simple life for ages amidst the Vedic traditions and culture in a tract that is most suited to agricultural pursuits. A rose is a rose by any name and why not join Shakespeare and say 'what is in a name?'

2

Is the Term 'Jat' Sanskritic in Origin?

The people who are called, and call themselves Jats today are no doubt, the most ancient Aryans, generally settled in north and north-west India. Many writers[1] have tried to prove their antiquity through the antiquity of their clan names, inseparably from the label Jat. In most cases the emphasis has been on the label, 'Jat' presuming it to be of Sanskritic origin. It is not necessary that if the people are ancient, their current label should also be equally ancient. But the temptation of tracing the label in sources, where it does not exist on the part of several amateur Jat historians, has led to great amount of confusion. The confusion has got worse confounded, especially at the hands of those who overtaken by their caste (label) patriotism have thrown to winds the regard for authentic historical facts and sound principles of research and linguistic investigation. In the case of several of such writers the label became more important than the people themselves. For them, ancient Sanskrit texts, particularly those of uncertain authenticity[2] came handy to yield, mixed with some imagination, the desired crop. The most favourite and sought after ally in the otherwise very uncertain Field has continued to be the Pāṇinian text *Jaṭa, jhaṭa sanghāte.* The text has been erroneously described as–*sūtra* of *ashṭādhyāyī* or a *śloka* or a phrase

1 Thakur, Desh Raj (Jat Itihas–in Hindi, 1934); Joon, Ram Swarup (History of Jats, Urdu/Hindi–1938, English–1967); Dahiya, B.S. (Jats: The Ancient Rulers, 1980); Pawar, Hukam Singh (The Jats: Their Origin, Antiquity and Migrations, 1993).

2 *Deva Samhita*–in Sanskrit, written in 18th/19th century,most likely commissioned to spread the absurd theory of the origin of Jats from the hair locks of Shiva.

in the *ashṭādhyāyī,* by most of such writers (who do not seem to do anything with Sanskrit), with generally faulty Roman transliteration, giving scope for miscarriage of intent. The effort of some writers in claiming to be precise by citing the reference number (3.3.19) of the text sought to be quoted from the *ashṭādhyāyī,* leaves one looking for the originally cited text only to land into an enigma, since the text at (3.3.19) is entirely different viz. *akartari cha kārake sanjnāyām*. Let us explain things:

The *ashṭādhyāyī* is a work of eight chapters, each having four quarters, where each quarter contains a number *of sūtras* arranged in a linguistically systematic and meaningful manner. The *sūtras,* individually and many a times in combination of several *sūtras* by inference, explain the formation of words of the Sanskrit language, as it was in Pāṇini's time. The *sūtras* deal with the raw material in the form of verbal roots *(dhātus)* by adding suffixes to obtain nominal and verbal forms of words. Pāṇini has identified and after appropriate classification put the verbal roots *(dhātus)* in a separate compilation, called the *dhātupāṭha.* Our two *dhātus* are listed at serial numbers 305 *(jaṭa)* and 306 *(jhaṭa–sanghāte)* in the *dhātupāṭha* with the simple meaning that each of the two is used in the sense of a cluster or a heap. The *sūtra* in the *ashṭādhyāyī* at 3.3.19 says that the suffix *ghan'* (having net value of 'a') comes after verbal stems when the sense of the root is denoted as having attained the completed state, e.g. *prāsah, āhārah* etc. However, the condition is that the (noun) word thus formed shall not be the one which can be used as an agent in the nominative case (in *kartā kāraka). But* our term *Jāṭa* (if we take it as a Sanskrit term) cannot be explained by the *sūtra* under reference, as it is very much used in the nominative case *(kartā kāraka).* Though words like jaṭā (hair locks), *jaṭah* (one having *jaṭa*) or *jaṭila* (one having intertwined hair) can be explained by other *sūtras*, the fact remains that Pāṇini has nowhere in his works mentioned the word *jāṭa* as such. If we wish to manufacture it retrospectively as a Sanskrit word of ancient ages Pāṇini's *sūtras* do not warrant it, the ancient Sanskrit literature does not reflect it. It is a pity that even some people, well versed in Pāṇinian grammar have failed to notice the true meanings of the references made. Bhim Singh Dahiya and Hukam Singh Pawar sound parochial in insisting that the term *jāṭa* has been deliberately obliterated from the ancient Sanskrit literature by the canny *brahmanas* for ulterior motives. Do they mean to say that the whole of Sanskrit literature has come from *brahmana* pen'? And if one were to accept Dahiya's thesis that almost all ancient rulers of India were Jats, how come that they as patrons of learning could have been so ignored by their court poets and other contemporary writers. Paradoxically both of them go on tracing the term *jāṭa* in various ancient Sanskrit texts where it does not exist.

Further, it may be pointed out that Pāṇini leaves little scope for mixing up of the meaning of the words '*sangha*' and '*sanghāta*', the former meaning an association of persons working for a common purpose, a corporation, a political unit or a group of living beings (*prāṇi samūha),* while the latter standing for a heap, cluster, accumulation, grouping, collection etc., generally of inanimate things, and of living entities, only when they give a monolithic appearance *(apraśṛṭavayavah samūha sanghātah) like* a herd of sheep *(avikaṭah). It* may also be mentioned here that Pāṇini has listed as many as twenty *dhātus* meaning *sanghāta,* all of which lead to the formation of nominal stems which convey the meaning of group, heap, combination or cluster of inanimate things.[3]

We also have a long history of the use of two words i.e., *sangha* and *sanghāta* in ancient Sanskrit literature, giving two distinct

3 Such dhātus are: *gośṭa; lośṭa; jaṭa; jhaṭa; piṭa; piḍhi; pūla; mṛkśa; vakśa; Śūla; Śroṇṛ; Ślokṛ; Śṭyai; styai; hudi (of bhvāāi gaṇa);and musta; pūla;pidi; Dapa;Dipa;ghaṭa (of churādi gaṇa) aśūnga; aśa (of divādi gaṇa).* Many words coming from these *dhātūs* conveying the meaning of cluster, heap or a monolithic combination can be observed in the modern Indian languages, e.g. *gośā* or *gośṭā*; *lothā*; *piṭaka*; *pinḍi*; *pūlī* or *pūlā* etc.

meanings as explained above.[4] Kautilya in his *Arthaśāstra* makes the same distinction between the meaning of *sangha* and *sanghāta.*[5] Therefore, the attempt on the part of several writers in first assuming the *term jāṭa* to be of Sanskritic origin and then trying to derive the same from the root *(dhātu) jaṭa* meaning *sanghāta,* and there after proceeding to construe it to convey the meaning of a political republic *(sangha) is* far-fetched and untenable. B.S. Dahiya and Hukam Singh Pawar have imagined the term *jāṭa* in the word *jāṭya* listed by Yaska (of the 8th century B.C.E.) in his etymological treatise *Nirukta* (1.14) among terms which had become obscure in their meaning with the passage of time. Explaining the term under reference Yaska states: "*jāṭya, Aṭṇāro i.e.* the *jāṭya means* a

4 Use of *sangha* for animates in the *Bhagvadgita: bhutaviśeśa-sanghān* (11.15); *mahrśi-siddha-sanghāh* (11.21)*; gandharva-yakśāsura-siddha-sanghāh (*11.22); *avanipāla-sanghaih* (11.26); *siddha-sanghāh* (11.36). Pāṇini's references to *Sangha* can be seen in the *sutras*: 1.2.13; 3.3.42; 3.3.86; 4.1.1 and 5.1.58. We get a sense from Pāṇini that *sangha* and *gaṇa* were synonymous terms. Yaudheya *gaṇa* is counted among *Ayudha-jīvi-sanghas*. The use of the term sanghāta for inanimates may be seen below: *upāya-sanghāta iva pravṛddha*–Raghuvansha, 14.11*; kṣata-setu-bandhano jalasanghāta ivāsi vidrutah*-Kumarasambhava, 4.6; *tuśāra-sanghāta-shilātaleśvapi*-Kumarasambhava, 5.55; ... *toyaugha-nikara-vrātavāra-sanghāta-sanchayāh*-Amarakosha-5.39. Also see Mahabharata (XII.298.17) for use of *sanghāta* for a heap or cluster: *sanghātavān martyalokah parasparamāśritah.*

5 i) Kautilya uses the term *sangha* in the sense of a corporation (*sajātādnyah sanghah*-2.1.32; *deśasya-Jātyāh-sanghasya dharmo-grāmasya vā mithah*-3.7.40; *tena jnāti-kula-sanghānām-3.10.45; jāti-sanghāschhidreśu prahareyuh-9.6.72; deśa-grāma-jāti-sangha-mukhyeśu*-13.5.9 and in the sense of a union of labourers (*tena sangha-bhṛtā vyākhyātāh* -3.14.12.; and in the sense of a confederacy of princes (*mitra-sanghasya vā yo antasthāyī tam labhet* -9.6.16; and in the sense of an oligarchy (*sangha-lābho danḍa-mitra-lābhānāmuttamah-11.1.1; viśiṣṭa-balābhāve sama-balaistulya-bala-sanghairvā balavatah sambhūya tiṣṭhet-7.15.3; viśeśataścha sanghānām sangha-dharmiṇām cha rājakulānām dyūta-nimitto bhedastannimitto vināśah..-8.3.64*

ii) Examples of *sanghāta* used in the sense of cluster, heap or combination or group. of inanimates in the Arthashastra: *pratisargamekārtha-charyām sanghātam cha varjayet-5.4.10; aśṭaproti sanghātya...iti naipālakam*-2.11.100 and also '2.14.17,26,30 *sanghātavān martyalokah parasparamāsritah* (Mahabharata, XII.298.17) wanderer (mendicant, presumably having matted hair). Both the above referred writers have gone far beyond this simple meaning, giving unbridled flight to their imagination. Dahiya has (hopefully, inadvertently!) altered the very text *Aṭṇāro* into *jāṭaṇāro* to instantly obtain the desired result i.e. *jāṭa*. This kind of argumentation is unacceptable. Hukam Singh on his part laboriously wades through a wide period of history, offering arbitrary and weird etymologies of the term, getting amusing at times. For sample, consider this: "*jāṭa* is called *Aṭṇāra* because he has blister folds (*Aṭaṇa* in modern Khadi Boli) on his feet." This is neither good linguistics nor good history. Hukam Singh's suggestion that the *jaṭā-pāṭha* of the vedic mantras could very well be taken as *jāṭa-pāṭha* (i.e., a recitation arrangement done by jats) surely will send any one having an idea of the vedic recitation system, into splits. Dahiya's penchant for marshalling Sanskrit and Prakrit texts, especially inscriptions in support of his thesis only reveals the inadequacy of his competencies in truly interpreting them. No right thinking person would like to go with him in tracing the Jats from demons like *Jaṭāsura* and *bāṇāsura* mentioned in the *Bṛhatsamhitā of Varāhamihira*.

Another favourite text of the proponents of Sanskritic connection of the term *jāṭa* is the disputable reading *ajayajjarto hūṇān'* in the Sanskrit grammar of Chandragomin of the 6th century C.E. in the context of illustrating the use *of Lang Lakāra* to denote an incident pertaining to immediate past. The alternative reading *ajayat gupto hūṇān* is supported by majority of scholars. However, even if we accept the former reading it does not help as the arguments advanced are based on assumptions. It is proposed by a section of scholars like K.P. Jayaswal (on whom Dahiya and Hukam Singh rely) that th*e jartah (=jāṭa)* here refers to Yashodharman, the Aulikara king who is referred to have defeated the *hūṇās* in his Mandasor Pillar Inscription. But this suggestion comes under cloud with the discovery, in 1983, of the Risthal (near Mandasor) Inscription (of 476 M.S. = 515 C.E.) of his father (?) Prakashadharman. The inscription clearly states that the latter defeated the *hūṇās* led by Toramana (Mihirkula's father). In any case the grammarian Chandragomin of 5th century C.E. could not have referred to a posterior event in the life of Yashodharman of the 6th century C.E. (vide his Mandasor Stone Inscription of Malava Samvat 589 (–532 C.E.). Moreover, deriving the term *jāṭa* from *jarta* arbitrarily, without putting the same in a chronological frame work remains merely a wild guess. We may also refer here to the futile suggestion of some writers who try to connect the vedic term *jaritā* with *jurta,* since the former simply means the singer of praise (of a deity). Equally untenable is the perambulatary derivation of the term *jāṭa from jnāti* via *jnāta* and *jata* offered by Thakur Deshraj in his painstaking work *Jat Itihas*. Mere incidence of the letters 'j' and 't' (no matter hard or soft) falling together in a term have led many a novices to jump to unwarranted conclusions, and ironically, welcomed in certain circles only offer examples of caste patriotism. But it becomes difficult even for a layman to stomach the assertion (as we find in the Devasamhitā) that the Jats owe their origin from the locks of hair of the mythical god Shiva, or for that matter the hair tuft of Virabhadra was the source of the Jats. Mythology should not be mixed with historical investigation. The domains of the two are entirely different.

So we have to reconcile and look for the antiquity of the people we are talking about on the strength of their clan names which occur in abundance in ancient Sanskrit sources including inscriptions, and for the moment, delink the label *jāṭa* for its own history and provenance to be researched separately. Pāṇini can be of great help as he has supplied us with a big list of *gotras* (clan names) in his *gaṇa-pāṭha* and also the *sūtras* dealing with *taddhita suffixes* in the *apatyādhikāra.* Having no success in tracing the term '*jāṭa*' in the Sanskritic or Indic sources, we should proceed to explore the possibility of the term having something to do with the Arabic/Persian connections of a much later period than hitherto believed. We should also ponder over the question why the term *jāṭa* has continued to carry a pejorative sense since the times we have noticed it being used for (or restricted to) a community which has ever stood for justice and truth as the saying goes, as also the fact that the term Jat transcends the meaning of a caste and is used in a general sense for describing people, language, food, colour or things, albeit in a pejorative sense.

3

Maharaja Surajmal (1707 A.D-1763 A.D)

The thoughtless bigotry and reckless economic policies pursued by Aurangzeb in contrast to the established tolerant approach of the Great Mughals was responsible for arousing the ire of the otherwise peaceful peasantry in the North and North-western India during the later part of the seventeenth century. The peasant revolt led by Gokula, though unsuccessful on the surface, proved a catalytic in igniting the minds of the peaceful village folk to fight for their rights. The eighteenth century brought bad omens for the Mughal Empire.

The demise of Aurangzeb in 1707 A. D. hastened its decline, inviting new players in the arena of politics, vying to occupy the space slipping from under the weakening Mughal throne. The same year (1707) gave to the peasantry of North India a son, like the sun risen on the horizon in the birth of Surajmal in the house of a peasant chief Raja Badan Singh of Bharatpur. Surajmal as a young boy joined his father as the latter's right hand man and helped in consolidating and expanding the Bharatpur territory to be ultimately recognized as a kingdom of consequence by the Mughal Emperor. With the deterioration of the sight of Badan Singh, Surajmal assumed the reins of the Bharatpur kingdom as a de-facto ruler. Moving on from where his father had reached, he acquired new territories for the Bharatpur State. But the hallmark of his approach was to restrict his endeavours in spreading his influence only over the territories largely dominated by his compatriots, the Jat peasants, who though of republican propensities accepted and went with the monarchical ruler. On his part Surajmal kept a peasant's profile both in dress and conduct. He had acquired the reputation of a warrior of great prowess at a fairly young age. His performance in the battle of succession at Baghru (1748) fighting from the side of Ishwar Singh of Jaipur lives on as a legend even today. Surajmal had risen to the occasion to fulfil his word given to the dying Raja Jai Singh. The powerful Marathas fighting on the side of the other contender Madho Singh had to taste dust in the rather fateful encounter. But at the same time Surajmal was well aware of the devastation that war brings to the common people. Therefore as far as possible he ensured that his territories do not turn into an arena of war. Internally he maintained law and order thoroughly assuring safety of the life and wealth of not only his subjects but also safe return of the wealth of traders which they preferred to deposit with Surajmal in times of turbulence. He continued to be helpful to the rising rulers of the peasant fraternity like Balram of Ballabhgarh, Rana Bhim Singh of Gohad and the jat rulers of Bajhod, Kajaura and Karauli.

How he handled, without giving up, the seize of his fort at Kumher (1754) laid by a confederacy of the Marathas, the Mughal Wazir Imad and the Rohilla chief Najib can be described as an incredible feat. He did not hesitate to part with his hard earned wealth to be given as war expenses to mighty opponents, be they the money seeking Marathas or the avaricious Afghan Abdali.

Surajmal's best talent came out in moments of crisis and turbulence. He kept his cool and baffled his contemporaries with his adroit diplomatic moves on many occasions precariously placed as he was between Abdali on the North and the Marathas on the South and he had to continuously deal with the established Rajputs. With his robust communication skills he succeeded in evading an invasion by Abdali (1757) who was lurking in the vicinity of Bharatpur after having devastated major parts of the Brij country side. The contents and tone and tenor of his letter to Abdali is seen by experts as an example of high diplomacy*. It is a matter of regret that but for the Marathas his efforts to form a coalition against Abdali bore little fruit. In not listening to his saner counsel the Maratha general Bhau had to pay a heavy price in the battle against Abdali at Panipat (1761).Surajmal indeed did not join the Marathas at Panipat because he had seen through their game. He had been forewarned by some well meaning elements around Bhau about his plan to swallow the Jat principality along with the Delhi throne once he was done up with Abdali. Surajmal was not a nitwit not to have seen through the Maratha's game.

Surajmal had all the qualities of a good ruler. Welfare of his subjects was his main concern. Trade and commerce thrived in his kingdom as he remitted transit duties and facilitated commercial transactions. He did not spend his money in wasteful projects but he did not lag behind in creating a full fledged department of charity under Somnath Chaturvedi. He patronized men of Art and Learning. The forts and buildings raised by him at Deeg, Bharatpur, Kumher and Wair are standing testimony of his taste as a builder and connoisseur of Art. His adopting of a happy blend of the features of Mughal and Hindu architecture in his buildings produced a new style called the Jat architecture. About his palace at Deeg which got completed several years after his death Father Wendell, a contemporary had this to say:

> "It is difficult to realize the expanse and magnificence of this palace without seeing it. I have seen none in Hindustan that would surpass it in magnificence, or would come near to it."

Surajmal was liberal in his religious views. He built several tanks, arbours, temples and chhatries at Govardhan, Mathura and Vrindaban and other places. He was equally regardful of Islam. When tauntingly asked by Malharrao, how the Jama Masjid at Mathura was proudly standing in his Hindu principality, he simply remarked that he could demolish it if some one could guarantee that no single temple would be dismantled as a consequence or more importantly if any one could guarantee him perpetual royalty, a fickle commodity. **His friendship with Safdarjung, was based on mutual faith and trust which stood all ordeals. Equally intense was his disliking and hatred for Najib.** In the words of Wendell, "He was loved by his own and respected by all near him not so much because of the exploits which he accomplished, as because he was forthright in his capability to do what he had taken upon himself."

The military legacy of Surajmal speaks of his organizing skills and vision of planning internal and external security for the people of his state. He left behind a cavalry of 15000 strength, 25000 infantrymen, 300 pieces of cannons with 60 elephants and 5000 horses in stables apart from a well endowed treasure.

It is however, a pity that Surajmal's last move in not heeding to Najeeb's pleadings for a reconciliation on the issue of the Mewati marauders betrayed Surajmal's Achille's heel. His going back on his word given to the Nawab of Farrukh Nagar was not in line with his entire polity. The slain Nawab's son amply guided and supported by Najib was lurking around looking for a suitable opportunity to take revenge.

Had Surajmal not been killed (25 December1763) with a stratagem in an ambush in east of Delhi at a time when victory was merely at a smelling distance the political map of India would have been differently drawn and the history of India differently written.

> *I have no important position and power in the empire of Hindustan. I am one of the zamindars living in the desert and on account of my worthlessness none of the Emperors of the age thought it worthy of him to interfere with my affairs. Now that a powerful Emperor like your Majesty, determined on meeting and opposing me face to face in the field of battle, would draw his armies against this insignificant person, that action alone would be discreditable to the dignity and greatness of the Shah and would help in the elevation of my position and would be a matter of pride for my humble self. The world would say that the Emperor of Iran and Turan had, out of extreme fear, marched his armies upon a penniless nomad. These words alone would be a matter of great shame for your Majesty… Moreover, the ultimate result is not altogether free from uncertainty. If with all this power and equipage, you succeed in destroying a weakling like, what credit there will be gained ?...But if by divine decree, which is not known to anyone, the affair takes a different turn (i.e. Ahmad Shah is forced to embrace defeat) all this power and predominance brought about

your Majesty during a period of eleven years will finish in a moment.

As to the threatening and violent order issued for the slaughter and devastation of myself, warriors have no fear on that score. It is well known that no intelligent man has any faith in this transient life. As for myself, I have already crossed fifty of the stages (of life) and know nothing of the remaining. There shall be no greater blessing than that I should drink the draught (of martyrdom)...in the field of battle with valiant soldiers and leave my name and that of my ancestors, on the pages of the book of the age to be remembered that a powerless peasant breathed equality with such a great and powerful emperor as had reduced mighty kings to subjection and that he fell fighting. And the same virtuous intention lies at the heart of my faithful followers and companions/ Even if I wish to make up my mid to attend at the threshold of your ...Court the honour of my friends does not permit me. Under such circumstances, if your majesty... forgive me... And turn your attentions to expeditions of greater importance, no harm shall come to your dignity and glory. The truth about the three forts (belonging to me), the object of your wrath, which have been regarded by your Majesty's chiefs as (weak as) spider's web, shall be tested only after an actual contest. God willing they shall be invincible as Alexander's Rampart.

[Quoted from *Tarikh-i- Imad-ul-Mulk, 243-245* by Ganda Singh, Durrani, 181-183]

You have not conquered India as yet. If you have taken hold of an inexperienced child (Imad) who held Delhi, what is there to be proud of? If you have any pretentions, why this delay (in attacking me) ?...I have spent large sums of money on this(Kumher) fort. The Shah can be kind to me by fighting with me as that the world may remember in future that a Badshah came from Vilayat and conquered Delhi, but was helpless against an insignificant *zamindar.*

[*Jam-i-Jahan Numa* quoted by Ganda Singh, Durrani, 183]

4

Sir Chhotu Ram - A Life to be Emulated

Mahajano yena gatah sa pantha|
Asare asmin sansare ko mrito na va jivati |
Sa *jato* yena *jatena* vansho yati samunnatim ||
Shreshtha yad yad acharate tadevetare janah |
Sa yat pramanam kurute lokastadanuvartate ||

On November 24, 2006 we observed the 125th anniversary of the birth of Chaudhary Chhotu Ram. The more remote in time we find ourselves from him the more closer he comes to the hearts and souls of many who for years toiled and slogged in the hope for living a better life free from exploitation of various sort. His ideas and ideals are relevant today more than ever before. When we look around the like of him is hardly seen.

Born in 1881 in a small nondescript village Garhi Sampla of Rohtak district of undivided Punjab, Chaudhari Chhotu Ram rose to be an important player in the political theatre of North West India during the first half of the twentieth century. Turning all disadvantages into advantages he graduated from St. Stephen's College Delhi with Sanskrit as one of his subjects securing second position in the University. Having impressed philanthropists like Seth Chhajju Ram of Hissar with his budding intellect Chhotu Ram managed to receive patronage from several quarters. His *Alma Maler* always stood by him. It is a coincident that the inaugural issue of the College Magazine 'The Stephenian' carried his article 'Improving Indian Village Life'. Even though Chhotu Ram had left the College he wrote the article on special invitation of the College Principal. He had a brief stint at Soks High school

Agra as a teacher. Here he published a small pamphlet on Physical Geography for high school students and another small book on Aids to the study of Indian history. While at Agra Chhotu Ram worked as honorary superintendent of Jat Hostel for a brief period and made several additions to it by raising funds for the same. Unwilling to take up the modest job of *Naib Tehsildar* he pursued law education and obtained LL.B. degree with first division from Agra University. He settled in Rohtak for practicing law in the district court after a brief stint in the service of the Raja of Kalakankar state and trying his hand in journalism editing the Hindi daily *Hindustan* started by the Raja in 1885. The Raja introduced Chhotu Ram to liberal politics and introduced him to Aurobindo Ghose and several other radical thinkers who visited Kalakankar. Rohtak turned out to be laboratory of experimenting with his egalitarian ideas and a testing ground for his organizing skills. He worked in tandem with Chaudhari Lal Chand and rose to become the President of the district Congress Committee of Rohtak (1916). He continued to fight for the cause of the peasants and the poor. The urban elite were alarmed at the growing popularity of Chaudhary Chhotu Ram and were always on the lookout for side tracking him from the political lime light. He patted company with the Congress in 1920 over the issue of non-payment of land revenue as a part of the non- co-operation movement launched at the Calcutta session of the Party. He had pointed out that the land of the defaulting farmers would be purchased by the very advocates of the movement when the same came to be auctioned under the law for recovery of government revenue. The non-land holding urbanites in the Congress could have no empathy with the farmers. Later Chaudhari Charan Singh took a similar stance when land revenue was sought to be believed abolished on holdings below a certain level in Uttar Pradesh.

The British administration in the district cultivated by the urban rivals of Chaudhary Chhotu Ram continuously harassed him to the extent of trying his trial for treason. He was however not deterred in his mission for working for the amelioration of the plight of the farmers and the poor. He fought in the high court and frustrated the attempts of the local administration in their efforts to get his license for practicing law cancelled and to get the land grants made in his favour revoked. Realising the role of an organization for political success in co-operation with other like-minded leaders he raised the Unionist Party representing largely the farming community among the Hindus, Sikhs and Muslims where economic interests were main concern. Religious difference did not come in the way. He toured extensively to awaken the masses to a path of economic freedom and communal harmony.

Chhotu Ram became a member of the Legislative Council of Punjab in 1923. His interventions in the debates in the house were taken with awed attention. Whenever he rose to speak serious stuff was expected, stuff which made a difference. His eloquence was full of intellectual content and his silence was meaningfully studied.

The secularists' consolidation under the flag of the Unionist Party achieved with the efforts of Chaudhary Chhotu Ram and like-minded Muslim and Sikh leaders ensured absolute majority for the Party in the elections to the Legislative council of the Punjab. The highlight of the results was the rout of the Muslim League which could manage to win barely two seats. Communal politics of Jinnah got a drubbing. The duo *of Chacha Bhatija* – Chhotu Ram and Khijra Hayat Khan proved more than a match to Jinnah's political machinations in Punjab. Alas! After the death of Chhotu Ram in 1945 it did not take more than a couple of years for Jinnah to turn the tables on the secularists and achieve the fragmentation of the country. Had Chhotu Ram lived a little longer and Jinnah's end had come when it came the political fortunes of India would perhaps have been different from what they came to be in 1947.

The high ethical values personally demonstrated by Chhotu Ram even in the murky world of politics for once raised the standard of politics to enviable levels. He would not enter into political alliances without commitment to principles and qualms. He did not allow personal considerations to come in the way of taking just decisions. He refused to oblige his personal friend Kanahhaiya Lal of village Matanhel even after the intervention of a common friend Shri Ghasi Ram for sanction of license for making

Khandsari though the later had suffered financial losses as a result of legislation relating to rural indebtedness passed by the Punjab Legislative Council. Another similar instance is not only Chhotu Ram's point blank refusal to help his child hood friend from his village Shri Lallu Singh in procuring a license for the import of huge quantity of rice from Sind to Punjab but also ensured that the license procured by questionable means was cancelled. However Chhotu Ram did not fail to reimburse the Rupees six hundred spent by Lallu Singh on his venture. Having experienced first-hand the urbanites' bias against the rural folk in general and the Jats in particular Chaudhary Chhotu Ram had a soft corner for the Jats and other deprived sections in the rural areas and did his best to ameliorate their sufferings. As a leader in the Legislative Assembly and as minister he took up the cause of the poor and worked for and put in place legislation which had far reaching impact on the lot of the deprived. He always based his arguments on facts and figures. He ably demonstrated how disproportionately high the quantum of annual indebtedness in Punjab amounting to Rupees Thirty Crore was to the annual revenue of a paltry Rupees Three Crore. Those who believed that Chhotu Ram's legislative measures were directed against the urbanites did not realize that out of 40,000 money lenders affected by measures regarding rural indebtedness 21,000 were from the class of zamindars with whom Chhotu Ram was clubbed together. The charge of discrimination was therefore born out of malice rather than based on sound logic.

Chaudhary Chhotu Ram put to shame many big people with his daily beauties. Throughout his career he offered bouquets of benevolence to the needy and the hapless. A few instances would give an idea of his mission in life. He had joined St. Stephen's High School at Delhi after passing the eighth class examination from Jhajjar. An obnoxious sweeper in the school hostel had continued to harass the students even after several complaints. The hostel superintendent did not pay heed to the issue. Young Chhotu Ram led a three weeks strike in the school. The striking students under the leadership of Chhotu Ram did not relent even on being evicted from the hostel. In the end the Principal intervened to accede to the demands of the students. The Raja of Kalakankar had invited

Chhotu Ram for a second stint to work as his Private Secretary and superintendent of education of his Principality. He had great liking for Chhotu Ram and asked the later to join him at dinner whenever any guest came (which happened quite often). One day when Chhotu Ram arrived at the table the dinner was half way through. Immediately after the dinner Chhotu Ram submitted his resignation. The Raja gave his explanation. Chhotu Ram stayed on. The Raja gave him six months' paid leave to prepare for Punjab Civil Service examination. A bright Sanskrit student doing his M.A. Sanskrit from Lahore came to know the name of the minister who had been financing his education only when he was getting ready to appear at the viva voce examination for entering the ICS. A western style suit had been ordered to be made for the young man. When he asked for the bill for making payment he learnt to his pleasant surprise that the bill had been already cleared by the minister who was non other than Chaudhary Chhotu Ram. When Mr. Chhotu Ram met the Financial Commissioner the latter an Englishman who knew Urdu expected that the former would address him as "*Huzoor*, *Mai Bap* etc." But Chhotu Ram spoke in chaste English. When asked why he did not speak in Urdu if he knew the language Chhotu Ram retorted, "but Mr. Walker (who was present at the meeting) does not know Urdu." Both the Englishmen were not amused. In the bargain Chhotu Ram got an offer for a junior post which he spurned. Very early as a child Chhotu Ram had demonstrated his how self-respecting he was. The village *bania* whom he visited along with his father offered a stool to his father but offered him the foot side of the bed to sit. Declining the offer Chhotu Ram kept standing till a separate stool was brought for him to sit upon. Maqbul Singh, a senior officer in the Punjab and who belonged to the *Chamar* community explained the reason for prominent display of a portrait of Chaudhary Chhotu Ram in his office room to Acharya Bhagawan Dev (latter Swami Omanand) when the later visited him sometime in the sixties thus; "I am here today but because of Chaudhary Chhotu Ram. He took me like his own son and financed my education and ensured for me a bright career. He is like a god for me. How can I forget him?" When the Chief Minister Sikandar Hay Khan at the bidding of the Governor, asked Chhotu Ram to go slow on the egalitarian legislation the later replied that the cabinet was not formed through the kindness of the Governor. Chhotu Ram was the only one to disagree with the suggestion of the Viceroy Lord Wavell for imposing control on the price of wheat at Rupees six a *maund* at a meeting of the food Ministers of States called in the wake of the Bengal Famine. When asked for reasons for his sole disagreement he explained that all other states were deficit in wheat. His was the only state in surplus of wheat. So he could not go against the interest of the farmers who would be sellers. The Viceroy was not pleased. When he spoke to the Chief Minister about Chhotu Ram's adamant stand the Chief Minister only said that as far as farmers 'issues were concerned Chhotu Ram was the Chief Minister. Chhotu Ram had suggested Rupees ten as the rate per *maund*. Eventually the rate of rupees eleven per *maund* was settled as the control price.

Though Chhotu Rant had left the Congress in 1920 he continued to have admiration and respect for Gandhiji. Before he would actually introduce any progressive piece of legislation, he would send the draft to Gandhiji for the latter's comment personally through Pandit Neki Ram Sharma of Bhiwani. As told by a correspondent (Mr. Madan Gopal) Gandhi Ji generally agreed with most of his legislative measures and not only blessed him but also asked him to go ahead. Gandhi Ji equally reciprocated and gave weightage to his opinion. Madan Gopal records, "When in 1942, Sir Sikandar Hayat khan proposed that a sentence be mentioned about protection to the Indian armymen (then called 'mercenaries') in the final draft of the statement on the conclusion of the Crips mission, Gandhi Ji agreed, subject to the condition that he would take Sikandar Hayat's word only if Chhotu Ram underwrote it. "Chaudhary Chhotu Ram's letter dated 15th August 1944 written to Gandhi Ji offering a classical critique of Rajgopalachari's formula for a settlement between the Congress and the Muslim League unfortunately remained unanswered. Perhaps there could be no answer to the arguments put forward by Chhotu Ram in his letter against the formula as it amounted to postponed partition of the country. However Gandhi Ji was gracious enough to acknowledge it after Chhotu Rams passing away in a letter of condolence dated 3rd February 1945 to Mrs. Chhotu Ram.

Persons like Chhotu Ram are born in centuries. The citadel of secularism built by him along with others till his death on January 9, 1945, remained unassailed by the continued onslaughts of communal forces led by Jinnah. He was a true *karmayogi* deeply inspired by the philosophy of the Bhagawad Gita. He was courage personified and a dare devil fighter for the cause of the farmer and the down trodden. The British government knighted him for serving the cause of the crown in the two world wars. The bonus was getting avenues of dignified employment opened for the much needy families of peasants. He became the great leader of his people–Rahbar-e-Azam. He stands tall as a role model for generations of young men and women among the farming communities of our country. He made the peasants free from the yoke of indebtedness but has left a heavy load of debt of his services to the community on our shoulders. We can free ourselves from the debt by emulating him in word and deed.

5

Working of the Gotra System Among the Jats

It is generally less known that the Jats, a peasant community in habiting the North and North West Parts of India are, among the best exemplars of true followers of the *Brahmanical* (Hindu) social order prevalent in India since time-immemorial. But it is pity that they have not received sufficient attention at the hands of scholars for the study of their ethnology. Being primarily agriculturists they had neither the inclination nor opportunities to prove their skills in accessing and consolidating political power in the Ancient times. Their self-sufficient economy, largely working under the barter system, was largely responsible for their living a contented and sedentary life. They were hardly concerned or worried about the affairs of the state. It was later in the medieval times, especially during the seventeenth and eighteenth centuries that the Jats asserted to carve out their position and establish their own political status. The house of Bharatpur was the Most prominent to form a state and get recognition from the Mughal emperor in 1742 A.D. under Badan Singh assisted ably by his son Surajmal. Earlier the Jats had surprised Changese Khan in the fourteenth century and Babar in the sixteenth century.

But essentially pursuing agricultural and pastoral occupations the Jats preferred to remain aloof from the humdrum of urban life and continued to live a sedentary life which was least affected by the shifting sands of time. They stood on the sturdy ground of the most productive tract of land ranging from the river Indus to the holy Ganges. It was this cradle of the ancient Indian civilization where they realized their life in full measure enriching the total social environment. Better known by their various separate clan names before acquiring along with many others, the collective nomenclature 'Jat' they scrupulously followed the traditions and customs developed under the common wealth known as the Brahmanical system governing the social and religious life of the people in the region.

Among the elements of the social organization the *gotra* system came to acquire an important place in very early times. In case of the Jats this system has continued to guide their life in a crucial manner. The republican minded Jats settled their social and political affairs through the Panchayat system. At micro level the *Khap-Panch*, always were, constituted of the representatives from villages of the same *gotra*. At micro level the *sarvakhap Panchayat* was formed by the representatives of all the *Khap panchayats*. The feeling of kinship being quite strong in a *gotra* it has been found to be an important element in forging brotherhood among its constituents, *Gotra* is a significant factor in regulating matrimony among the Jats in accordance with the well thought out parameters of prohibitions and eligibilities relating to the would be couples.

Before proceeding further it would be better to understand the meaning and nature of *gotra*. But since *gotra* itself has its genesis in the familial/ kinship circle (*sapinda*) we may take up the later for explaining first what *sapinda* stands for. *Sapindata* is reckoned on three occasions, *viz*, first for determining a prohibition in relation to marriage, second for determining the line of succession mentioned in a will, and third in determining the persons who were to perform the purificatory rites after impurity effected through cases of birth or death. According to the dominant view expressed by the Mitakshara school sapinda is one who has body elements common with another, Father and children, grand-father and grand-children; mother and mother's father; uncles and their wives, wife and sister in-law all fall in the category of *sapindas*. In this way the whole universe would become *sapindas* of any one. To limit this infinity of *sapindata*, Yajnavalkya gave seven generations on the father's side and five generations on the mother's side as the limits of *sapindata*. Marriage among *sapindas* was prohibited. Such prohibition being on a personal and limited scale the *gotra* system in the manner of labelling was brought into play for determining the prohibitions on a more wider and general way. Persons of the same *gotra* had a common ancestry going back to several generations The commonality could be traced to place of residence, some family trait, a nick name or a title or even a common *Rishi*. In the context of kinship identity *gotra* has been mentioned by the famous Sanskrit grammarian Pāṇini (5th-6th century B.C.) and commented upon by the author of the Kashika Vritti (4th-5th century A.D.) on Pāṇini's work- *the Ashtadhyayi*. In Pāṇini's time, *gotra* was synonymous with family or *kula*. In the sutra–'apatyam pautraprabhriti gotram' (3-1-62) he states that the progeny from grandson onwards would be called *gotra*. A large number of name of *gotras* among the Jats of the modem times ending in the suffix aryan such as kakrayan, salklayan, kadyayan thakrayan etc. fit into Pāṇini's definition of *gotra*. Another sutra of Pāṇini 'vriddhasya chapujayam' (4-1-16) is years reflected in the eldest son and heir of the family representing it at Meetings of assembly of elders. Pāṇini calls this heir by the technical name *gotrapatya* and those younger to him as *yuvapatyas*.

The working of the *gotra* system among the Jats for contracting marriages before the beginning of the last century was marked by four fold prohibitions of *gotras* of the contracting parties, *viz*. (i) the *gotra* of the groom's father (*pita*); (ii) that of the mother's father (*mata*); (iii) that of the father's mother's father (*dadi*); and (iv) that of the mother's mother's father (*nani*). None of these four should tally with any of the similar four in case of the bride. These prohibitions take care of the prohibition of *sapindas* also to a great extent. The prohibitions could be reduced in number by the caste Panchayat on exigency of situation. Adding to the above prohibitions some sections of Jat *gotras* form together one exogamic group in the belief that they are related to each other by kinship. The group comprising Dalai, Rathi, Maan and Dabas *gotras* are an example of this phenomenon. It is possible that this grouping is a vestige of the *Pravara* system under which the constituent *gotras* of a *Pravara* practised exogamy. Alternatively geographical proximity of these *gotras* working on the principle of *seemjod biradari* (kinship of proximity) could be responsible for the grouping. It could be described as the brotherhood of *gohand* i.e. a place upto which the cattle (*gau* or *go*) of a particular village would be roaming about (from the Sanskrit root hand) for grazing. The cow connection of *gotra* is sought to be traced by some scholars as a basis of forming *gotras*. The practice of kinsmen of several generations keeping a common- *gotwara/gitwara* or cow yard is cited as a dimension to be taken into account for deciphering the true import of *gotra*. We are also not unaware of the pattern of formation of cattle (cow) herds in the villages of yesterday. Even cattle herds were seen to have been formed on the basis of kinship Clusters of families.

Already there are signs of the above mentioned prohibitions on their way out as match making especially among educated young professionals settled in big cities and other urban conglomerations is getting difficult day by day. The prohibitions appear quite teasing to the young generation. Perhaps they need to know a little more about ethnic issues. Notwithstanding the expansion of means of transport and communications the average distance between the contracting parties is getting reduced for ensuring easy and frequent interaction between the families on either side, The narrowing down of choices for finding grooms has led to the deletion of the two last numbered prohibitions in quite a few places as the situation demanded. No formal Panchayat decisions are known to have been taken in such cases. Modernity is overtaking tradition in quite a subtle manner.

Gotra comes into reckoning during marriage ceremonies. For a last stage check *gotras* of the side of the groom as well the bride are recited at the main ceremony. At the ceremony of farewell (*vida*) each side of the parties contracting marriage amid other things, offers token money as honour to any one married to a woman of their respective *gotra* present among the opposite side. This honouring goes beyond the venue of the ceremony as far as women are concerned. The groom accompanied by several others interested goes round the village looking for all women of his *gotra* to offer them money as a token of honour. In turn all the members of his entourage get treated to a drink of sweetened hot milk. The kinship bonding thus gets further strengthened. It indicates also the kinship of milk–*doodh* and *poot* have a strong connection in kinship in the eyes of a Jat. Village settlements mainly constituting Jat population are characterized by a predominant *gotra* Members belonging to the main *gotra* are called *khede ki doob* and the head originally marked for habitation is called *Kheda*. The *gotra* of the original inhabitants becomes the *gotra* of the *Kheda*. Persons of other *gotras* may have settled later. Even if the former are reduced to a minority the *gotra* of the *Kheda*–remains unaltered. Guests are welcome but only as long as they remain guests. They are not welcome as proprietors. The Hindu succession Act of 1956 giving daughters equal rights in parental land was a welcome measure in as much as it did away with gender bias and served as an ameliorating measure for many a sad stories of disinherited daughters having no brothers to look after them. But among the Jat the working of the above law has been beautifully skirted aside by the willing connivance of sisters who voluntarily and happily opt out of the succession line in the larger interest of maintaining a strong kinship relationship for generations to come. The Jats give the rationale for this strategy with the plea that the sister's husband of a different *gotra* owning land in the *Kheda* of his wife's *gotra* would sow seeds of another *gotra* in the same village thus weakening *gotra* bonding. Further a question is asked as to what happened to the land already owned by the sister's husband in his ancestral village? Of course, there are cases known where the progeny of the immigrating family decided to acquire the *gotra* of the *Kheda* to steer clear of many functional difficulties only to throw up peculiar complications in distant future. We are aware of a recent case how a Rathi family migrating to and, in due course of time, adopting the new *gotra*, Hooda fell prey to the hawkish eye of the *gotra* zealots.

A girl of the family married to a boy of Dahiya *gotra* in a village having Rathi as the Kheda gotra had to go through harrowing time before the matter could be finally resolved to the satisfaction of all concerned including the caste *Panchayat* though not before the matter reached the High Court of Punjab and Haryana and the State Government made its stand clear on the issue. It may be mentioned here that the two families concerned had organized the marriage after taking into consideration all the aspects of the prohibitions under the *gotra* system. The *Shastras* also support the settlement arrived at. Were there a marriage contracted between *sago-tras* in ignorance of the facts it would be deemed to be annulled forthwith which was not the case in the instance cited above. Among the Jats the phrase '*gotra milna*' is a polite way to signify dissolution of a marriage. In any case, the modern law protects the new generation against all customary practices and the choice is theirs'. However, at the same time we cannot shut our minds from thinking about the sociological dimensions inherent in the situation. Probably the fragmentation and reduction in size of land holdings in the backdrop of employment opportunities opening up in diverse sectors a fresh look is needed in relation to the whole question of land rights and succession laws, the Jats, in any case, are pragmatic and magnanimous enough to find their own ingenious solutions to the issues visiting them in the modern times.

6

The Veil Unveiled

A couple of years back an Australian Muslim cleric almost lost his job for advocating the use of veil in his own puritanical way of pointing out how women not properly clad invited potential rapists as would uncovered meat a cat. He had to run for cover in giving explanation for what he had really meant by his remark. If that would not satisfy the liberals among the Australian Muslims the cleric proceeded on indefinite leave. On the heels of the above incident the Imam of Delhi came calling Shabana Azmi by her professional name in some derogatory terms (that *nachane gane wali aurat!)* for her very innocent and considered observation that 'the Quran only says that a women should properly cover her body and that the holy book nowhere prescribes the veil in any form as a compulsory wear'. Shabana, an eminent and intellectual Muslim woman found over whelming support for her observations among all intellectual circles including Muslims. I believe in both the cases it was not so much the content of the remarks but perceived connotations that were behind the ruffled reactions in both the instances. In the first case one cleric was prescribing a crude remedy to a healthy person and in the second case another cleric felt threatened of some one trying to 'poach' his chickens from the yard he so zealously keeps guarding. The casualty was a serious debate on the veil, its origin, its use and relevance in a given context. The media, for obvious reasons, did stage some discussion under controlled conditions. Thus different sides of the veil remained unveiled. It is generally believed that the veil is specific to Muslim women only and that the *purdah* system prevalent among vast sections of non-Muslim women, especially in north and north-west India has Muslim links, albeit in uncomplimentary terms. It is therefore a compelling subject to comment upon in its historical and sociological aspects. Pronouncing sweeping judgments one way or the other is, of course, a tricky affair.

First let us take the case of the Arab world. The desert countries have their normal dress suited to the environmental conditions. The long cloak is the normal outer cover to take the onslaughts of the sandy winds. A suitable head cover is also in place. The outfit has become a national dress flaunted proudly at ceremonial occasions even in strange lands. The version meant for women is not much different. So it is easy to understand that the veil has its origins in necessity. Necessity is best met when it takes the form of a custom and gets religious sanction. Therefore we have the Quranic reference regarding the need to cover the body properly. It can be argued that if environmental considerations don't warrant the wearing of a veil why should one insist for the same. The answer is that if a Muslim woman wants to wear it then why not. But beyond that the sociological aspect must also be taken into consideration. Let us admit that the Muslims for historical reasons are possessive about their women (who else is not any way?). Endogamous system of marriage among Muslims and religious sanction for polygamous marriage are important factors to be taken into account before evaluating their attitude towards their females in general. A superficial view of the Muslim attitude in such matters on the part of their non-Muslim compatriots does not help in arriving at a correct understanding of the whole matter. Moreover, as a minority community the Muslims in India, in order to maintain and assert their identity, tend to huddle together clinging to their religious symbols and practices which their counterparts in Muslim countries hardly need or care to adhere to. We daily notice similar phenomena in many manners among caste groups of the Hindu society, of course with difference in emphasis.

Let us now try to explain the phenomena of *purdah* among the Hindu women of north and north-west India. It will not be entirely true to say that the custom of *purdah* among the Hindu was a Muslim contribution. Though we do not have reference to *purdah* in the Rig Veda we do have mention of the same in Indian literature much before the birth of Islam. The *Aitreya Brahmana*

(12.11) mentions that the bride feels shy in the presence of her father-in-law and leaves hiding herself. Such behaviour, more than anything else is indicative of respect for the elders, especially in the new home of the father-in-law. Then we have Pāṇini in his *Aśṭadhyāyī* (3.2.26) talking about *asuryampashya* women who remain confined indoors obviously for reasons of strict privacy. Such women perhaps belonged to the higher ruling classes and were not generally exposed to public gaze. In *Ayodhya Kanda* of *Valmiki's Ramayana* (33.8) we find comments with lament on the turn of fate of Sita following Rama marching openly on the roads in contrast to her former status when even the celestial beings could not glance her. Such cases could hardly be taken to throw much light on the custom of veil. But Draupadi's statement in the *Mahabharata* (Sabhaparva (69.9) that 'the Kauravas have broken a time honoured tradition of not taking married women to public gatherings or meetings) gives a clue to some dimensions of the custom *of purdah.* Kalidasa in his immortal drama *Abhijnanaśakuntalam* (5.13) shows Shakuntala entering the court of her husband Dushyanta covering her face with a veil, which she removes only when compelled to talk face to face with him to establish her identity. In the *Harṣacarita of Bāṇabhaṭta* there is a reference to Harsha's sister Rajyashri covering her face with a red cloth at the time her future husband Grahavarma came to see her for the first time. Elsewhere in the same book Bana Bhatta refers to veiled women of Sthaneshvara (Thanesar in Haryana). In the *Kadambari* of the same author Patralekha is depicted wearing a veil *(avagunthana)* of red colour. Bhasa, a predecessor of Kalidasa in his play *Svapnavasavadattam* (Act VI.) speaks of *kalatradarshanarha jana*, from whom a married woman should not hide herself, implying that there could be category of persons before whom married women did not appear. Here in we find a clue to the protocol of observing *purdah* among married women in north and north-west India. That the women of the nobility moved out of their homes with veil on can be inferred from a remark of Vachaspati Mishra (9th century A.D.) in his *Sankhyattvakaumudi.* Following the custom for centuries all Women over vast areas of north and east India irrespective of their age observe *purdah!* avoid appearing before male members except in the following cases :

(i) All unmarried girls living in their paternal homes or appearing elsewhere.

(ii) All married women irrespective of their status or age living in their paternal homes or appearing before men of their father's *gotra* or their mother's father's *gotra* and other relations from the mother's or father's side. {A married woman in this case would not appear before visiting males from her in-laws' place of *gotra* in whose presence she would have to observe *purdah*. This disappearance act was resorted to for the purpose of maintaining the exemption from the condition of observing *purdah* at her father's place.

(iii) All married women appearing before males younger in age and not higher in relationship hierarchy on the side of the husband.

(iv) All married women irrespective of their marital status or age appearing before total strangers far away from their marital homes in neutral areas not falling in the area or her in-law *gotra*.

Women of many families under the influence of Arya Samaj, and by following the example of the urban elite, and with the spread of education among women have given up the practice of observing *purdah* (largely in urban areas). No social or caste censure or sanction is entailed in such cases. But when these very women move to visit the traditional homes of the in-laws in the remote rural areas the *purdah* norms come into play in some measure.

Where ever *purdah* is observed it may take an appropriate form as follows:

(i) *Ghungat* is the lowering of the head-scarf from the front so as to cover the face of the woman completely. It is observed on formal-occasions. To make the picture more perfect the corner of one end of the head scarf passing across her front is tucked on the opposite side of the string of the skirt.

(ii) *Ohala* is covering of the face on the side in an angle sufficient to cover the face so that it is not visible from the side of the concerned male member.

(iii) *Palla* is a symbolical drawing of the head scarf over the face to show respect to the concerned male member.

(iv) *Dhattha* is the covering of the face in the manner of a masque leaving the area over the eyes uncovered for visibility. It is resorted to mostly during agricultural operations to keep both the hands free and to protect the lace from dust and other pollutants. In the process the female members enable themselves to keep a veiled distance from those whom they should avoid coming face to face.

It may be observed that the *purdah* is in some way related to the four *gotra* system of endogamy of caste and exogamy of *gotra* among most communities in India, especially the Jats. It has its use and necessity in the rural society where the joint family still continues to be in practice and where communication among male and female members is also governed in the manner of the *purdah.* It is not so much of a restriction on the freedom of women as much as it is a medium of expression of condescension and regard for the seniors in age on the husbands side and hierarchy of relationships without the loss of female bashfulness.

Lastly we may claim to be surrounded by the use of *purdah* or veil in abundant measure in our daily life and language cliché. Thus we daily hear of veiled threats traded among men and women of all persuasions. There is no dearth of people who would hasten to put *purdah* on all that was evil. The world of Hindi cinema does not feel exhausted with an exhaustive use of the term *purdah* to embellish its lyrics. Modern living can't simply do without draping itself albeit on the gaping holes. You call it by any name *veil, purdah, naqab, sihab or chadar or curtain* but you must draw it if you wish to call it a day. There is no use of talking, of its uses and abuses. So let us live with it and live with those who observe it.

7

Cast of the Caste Mould - An Obverse View

Indian society with the exception of the tribal component has been living, since time immemorial, in caste groups which normally derive their nomenclatures from the occupation they pursued. Occupations with rare exceptions being hereditary caste also came to be hereditary. Even the change of profession on the part of a person would not lead to the change of his or her caste. The position continues to remain the same till his death. The same is largely true also of the religion of a person. One inherits at least the nomenclature of the religion followed by his parents. But the choice of change of religion is always open. On the other hand Indian history is replete with cases of en-mass change of religion by conversion to Islam or Christianity voluntarily or under duress and/or by force or through temptations of various sorts.

Castes have through the centuries proliferated into sub castes with the proliferation of occupations and vocations. Hierarchy among the castes also developed based on the relative importance of the occupation/vocation in the life of the community as a whole, the locale or the strength of population of a particular caste. However, the Brahmins have invariably enjoyed precedence in the set up irrespective of their economic status or minority in number obviously for the reason of their association with learning as its propagators or custodians and saviours through oral tradition where written words went into flames through fire of invading foreign hordes on in-numerous occasions. But all along there has been an element of inter dependency among the various castes assuring dignity and sense of fulfilment to all. Of this we would talk a little later. Now let us consider the relationship of caste with the ancient *Varna* system.

It is generally held and believed that the *Varna* system was as old as the Rig Veda and that the caste system was a by- product of the same through multiplication of the *Varnas* under a process of exogamy of the obverse and reverse type or through the total breakdown of the code of marriage among the various *Varnas (varnasankara).* This view happily is not shared by several enlightened indologists like Mahamahopadhyaya P.V. Kane and modern sociologists like G.S. Ghurye. Kane in his History of the *Dharmashastras* has aptly pointed out that the code of matrimony in ancient India was characterized more in observance than in its violation. Ghurye in his classic work *Caste and Race in India* has candidly described the *Varna* system as imaginary (notional). *Jati,* the Sanskrit word for caste is generally derived from the verbal stem *jani (jan–to take birth)* pointing to its hereditary nature.

What good the caste system has served our society cannot be fully fathomed unless we imagine what would have happened to us without it. But for the present it may be useful to delve upon the reverse side of the mould of the caste System. The perpetual Brahmanic hegemony in social hierarchy abetted by the unscrupulous rulers ever in search of legitimacy for their ill-gotten thrones militated against the very postulates for which the Brahmins themselves stood in the vedic age. The hitherto not so unimportant service class was sought to be divided and denied of rights which were theirs by nature's law. To perpetuate their degradation, new codes were drawn to give religious sanction to some of the very inhuman acts done against the down trodden. The practice of untouchability combined with the denial of right to education to certain sections of the society gradually turned out to be the scourge of the caste system. To say this is not to deny the relentless work done both in word and deed on the part of the saints like Chaitanya, Ramanuja, Kabir, Guru Nanak and many others who preached in the vernaculars for the social uplift of the downtrodden.

As mentioned above the obverse side of the caste mould in our traditional rural society needs to be highlighted to understand its intrinsic strength so that propelled by our impulsive reflexes we may not, in the manner of throwing the baby away along with the bath water, incur the folly of joining the chorus for abolition of caste. To recount the good done by the caste system and being done even today we may refer to a few positive features of the system. The first and foremost is the matrimonial solutions offered under it for centuries till the present times in the largely rural and far from modernized population. The level of service offered by caste match makers and the judicious settlement of matrimonial disputes by the caste elders are indeed indispensable even in the modern times. No doubt the contentious part of it in denying consenting couples from contracting marriage outside the fold of their caste is slowly dying its own death for the better health of the system. The second notable feature was the interdependency of castes leading to healthy communal relations. The farmers, for example, depended upon the workers from landless castes for the timely and efficient harvesting of their crops and the workers on their part felt obliged to get from the farmers wages in the form of harvested crop proportionate to the amount of work done. Same was the case of members of castes like potters, carpenters, blacksmiths, barbers etc. who got a fixed measure of grain from each of the farmers in their respective beat *(jajmani)* in the village in lieu of supplying pots; carrying out minor repairs of agricultural implements; ironing out the ploughshare and the triangular cutter *(kartaki)* of the plough and other iron implements; providing hair cutting and shaving solutions to male clients in addition to serving as master of ceremonies at marriages and providing through their women folk hair management and make up solutions for women clients respectively from families *(jajman)* allotted to each-a smooth and efficient system indeed involving no cash transactions so infested with cuts and levies of the modem times like the nagging service tax. The village washer man fell in the same category. On the spot transactions, generally in cash, were practiced in case of services like those rendered by the goldsmith, the bangle man, the tailor, the shoe maker etc. The scavenger was a class apart. His family got cooked food daily in the morning to be collected pro rata from each family in his beat *(jajmani)* in lieu of services rendered for disposal of the daily household waste and management of animal dung and for brooming the respective environ. Interestingly the scavenger appeared in an entirely new avatar when he assembled others of his caste to form a Band of music players at marriage processions. He got his fees in cash for the service rendered in such cases. He also acted as the fuel man at the small sugarcane crushers and was also responsible for the management of the sugarcane waste like begasse *(khohi)* and press mud *(maili)*. The shoemaker i.e. the *Chamar* was available for giving a helping hand to the farmer in many ways. He took responsibility for disposal of the dead animals. The animal hide obtained in the process was his wage with bonus one could say. He sometimes took responsibility for rearing a female buffalo calf of a husbandman till she grew up into age of reproduction on the basis of sharing fifty percent of the valuation arrived at mutually. In some cases he would enter, into a contract of working as the ploughman against twenty percent of the produce. Such arrangements were observed in the families of farmers who had depleted male workforce or who had ample produce to share. The non-farming communities in a village utilized one another's services on a reciprocal basis. The system of interdependency was at the core of our life since ages. The vedic householder offered prayers and made oblations to gods to get in return all the wealth and riches in cash and kind and in addition good health and desired progeny. The same mutuality of interests and reciprocity is echoed in *Śrīmadbhāgavadgīta* (III. 11). It is a pity that with such a great tradition of caste playing a positive role it degenerated into a vehicle for oppression and denial of justice to the deprived. But at the same time all ills of society can not be attributed to one single factor. The bitter truth is that in the process of fragmentation of traditional institutions under foreign yoke, caste also slumped into slumber and failed to rise to the occasion when circumstances demanded. Thus on India getting freedom as a result of the national upsurge all caste relations appeared to be shaking. However, the orthodox elements and the progressive ones differed in approach to tackle the ills of the caste system. One school of thought was for reverting to the imagined ancient four *Varna* system. Ghurye reminds us of Gandhiji having advocated such an approach early in his political career albeit without fuller details of the procedure for achieving such a social order. Equally utopian was another suggestion pleading for the progressive amalgamation of sub-castes into one caste on the basis of cultural commonality and economic similarity. After such castes reach approximate equality there could be further amalgamation. The process could go on till a casteless society was achieved. The third school of thought stood for its total abolition on grounds of several of its feature being degrading and obnoxious. Sixty years of struggle brought us freedom but an equal number of years of self-governance has not succeeded in bringing about a casteless society. On the contrary caste patriotism has given place to caste-ism. Caste- ism at social level has declined considerably but narrow caste-ism is becoming a hall mark of our political life. Exclusiveness is the characteristic of newly emerging identities. Our joint achievements are sought to be deconstructed for claiming credit for separate identities. And this, is happening in almost all domains of our life. There is a caste-based proliferation of charitable, cultural and educational Trusts and caste welfare associations. Now we have caste hospitals, roads named after persons highlighting their caste identities. Caste based reservations originally conceived to end after a limited period of affirmative action do not seem to achieve the stated objective of dispensing social justice even in infinity of time. There are clamorous claims being made on behalf of different caste groups in various states to get included in the lists of castes granted reservations. All this is happening when our successive governments irrespective of their avowed political ideology have been fiercely engaged in the almost impossible task of removing all caste inequalities among our people. The problem is that we are trying to handle the horse by trying to twist its tail and getting hurt in the process. Experienced cavalrymen would tell us that we need to hold the horse from the front and ride it for benefit keeping balance. Kin feeling is a natural instinct. Caste feeling is a slight extension of kin feeling. Therefore to tackle caste distortions we have to first recognize its reality and then proceed to harness it in the context of interdependencies and mutuality of interests and pooling of strengths rather than denounce it without being able to renounce it. Let us recognize the obverse side of the coin of caste and dust the mould into which it is cast.

8

Customised Matrimony, Endogamy/ Exogamy: Challenges of Modernity

Day after day we hear reports of young couples in north and north-west India losing their lives for marrying in contravention of caste (endogamy) or *gotra* (exogamy) rules, ironically, at the hands of their very near and dear kinsmen who take pride in giving their heinous act the name of 'honour killing'. Cases of young couples mysteriously disappearing without any trace, soon after they secretly married crossing the caste and *gotra lakshmana rekha* should fall in the same category as presumably they either ended their lives on their own or were put to the sword by their own leaving no clue of the hoary act. The same region is reputed to have shown a very low ratio of females vis-a-vis male population per thousand over the centuries giving reasonable quarter for suspecting of the prevalence of the condemnable practice of female foeticide. Peasant communities here, not denying the latter practice offer a number of alibis, which however do not go to justify the practice. These are not ordinary crimes against humanity but fall in the category of sinful acts which await retribution in after life also apart from whatever exemplary punishment law should be able to impart. But having said that one cannot deny the intricacies involved in the issue. Nor it is enough to describe the phenomena merely as one of tribal psyche and lack of education failing to march with modernity and clinging to custom in disregard of the state law simply for the reason of its prevalence among the rural communities. Therefore there is a need to go a little deeper into the causes and background of the incidents. The role of the caste *Panchayats* also needs to be constructively understood in this context.

A few typical cases, may be cited to describe the scene. We may first mention cases where the norm of endogamy (marriage within one's own caste) was reported to have been violated. Reported from inner rural areas of Uttar Pradesh, Haryana and Punjab from time to time, with a disturbing regularity, these are cases where invariably the girl of a higher caste had eloped with and married a boy of some *Dalit* caste. In the manner of a set pattern the couple in each case was apprehended, tied to a tree alive and lit with fire ending their dreams and lives in smoke. The hapless parents and kinsmen of the boy in almost all cases remained mute spectators while the men of the girl's side inflated by the heat of the moment gloated over their kill, taking pride in vindicating their 'honour' to the satisfaction of the traditional caste *Panchayat*. In several cases the boy and the girl contracting marriage voluntarily were reported to be hailing from the same village. Though no direct violation also of the rule of marrying only outside their *gotra* (exogamy) had occurred in these cases but for the reason of marrying a girl of the same village there was in each case violation of the extreme type of the rule of neighbourhood kinship (*seemjod biradari*). Notwithstanding the sanction of law these marriages were not found tenable for the simple reason that in the tract under reference a daughter of a village cannot be socially accepted as a daughter-in-law at the same time in the same village. The lifestyle of the rural communities does not countenance such a situation. It can happen in urban settlements where anonymity and disguised identity can help overcome the attending dilemmas arising from contentious marriages. But the couple would never be welcome in the house of the parents of the girl. The progeny that they beget would take the caste of their father. Kinship relationship between the two families would end forever.

Same is true in cases of violation of the rule of not marrying within one's own *gotra* (exogamy). Violation of the rule of exogamy is further compounded if the couple belonged to the same village and had a common *gotra* in addition. Their fulfilling the condition of endogamy would be of no avail. The *Dharmasūtra*s support the view that marriage in the same *gotra* is invalid. The reported stand of the caste *Panchayats* was in the context of maintaining a healthy social order in a given environment. Doesn't law essentially base itself on such postulates? And has not the principle of separate law for specialized or differently situate groups been recognized by the Apex court on more than one occasion? Plurality of a society needs plurality of dispensations for regulating its life in a harmonious manner. There was a case widely reported in the print and electronic media last year. A daughter of the Hooda *gotra* had married a boy of the Dahiya *gotra* in a certain village in Haryana. The girls' family originally belonged to the Rathi *gotra* but had migrated to a village of the Hooda *gotra* several generations back and had adopted the same as their *gotra*. The fact that the village where her prospective in-laws belonged had a sizable (almost half of the village) population of Rathi *gotra*, was overlooked at the time of settling the marriage. Nearly a year later the happy married life of the couple was traumatized by the caste *Panchayat* mobilized by the Rathi faction of the village on the sly that the girl actually was of *Rathi gotra* and that her marriage in a village almost half of which had Rathi as their *gotra* was untenable. The girl's husband went through very trying time under pressure of the *Panchayat* for annulling the marriage by having a *rakhi* tied by her on his wrist proclaiming a new relationship of a brother and a sister between them. His married sister, an educated and well informed lady stood by him and his wife giving them needed shelter and support in every manner. The intervention of the High court and alert action on the part of the government combined with a positive role played by the electronic media saved the situation. Several well -meaning people in the village also intervened to placate the *Panchayat* by producing documentary proof in support of the girl's parents having adopted the new *gotra*. It may be mentioned here that there are cases galore of similar nature which have gone unnoticed and undetected.

It may not be out of place to point out here the declining fortunes of *gotra* as a parameter of prohibition in matrimony. Tradition and caste *Panchayats* themselves have pragmatically been reducing the number of prohibited *gotras* for contracting marriage for centuries. And in the recent years communities at several places have gone ahead without the sanction of the caste

Panchayats to further reduce the number of prohibited *gotras* to ensure that match making does not become a big problem. The *gotra* of mother's mother's father was out from the list more than a century back. It is not known if a decision to this effect was taken in a formal way by a caste *Panchayat.* Today the list of prohibited *gotras* in most places is two only after dropping father's mother's father's *gotra*. What effectively remain now as prohibited *gotras* are that of mother's father and one's own father-quite a climb down from the original seven in the list.

There is no denying the fact that modernity has been a contributory factor, firstly in breeding the problems and then providing tools to fight against tradition and custom on the basis of law and reason. But at the same time modernity being not a villain also offers solutions for the willing. Modern means of transport and communication have led to the unsolicited contact between people on a more frequent basis than one could imagine some years ago. Boy meets girl is no more a phenomena on the silver screen only or is limited to the city street. Rural life is not untouched by it. It has become a small world indeed. Spread of education, break-up of the joint family and shifting of traditional occupations have among other things opened, both for men and women, doors to enter the vistas of self-realization. The small screen having entered almost every home even in the rural areas has had its toll in influencing the young boys and girls to challenge tradition and custom wherever and whenever they find it obstructing their course chartered under the inspiration received from non traditional and custom free channels especially when tradition and custom have almost lost the race to modernity on several fronts. It is not claimed here that traditional society has always been a paragon of virtues. It is also not denied that clandestine relationships were not unknown in traditional societies. What is being emphasised is that tradition and custom keen to receiving adherence was equally willing and courageous in educating the young the fuller meanings of social life, family and relationships. Creating awareness of personal obligations and duties was more important than awareness of personal rights and privileges. And no wonder tradition and custom remained beacons of light for the society for several millenniums as we know. It is not that tradition and custom have remained static. Our long history is a history of social changes as reflected in our *Smriti* literature and achievements in several other fields. We have to rise to the occasion and find the golden middle path once again which we traversed whenever faced with dilemmas in our social life. But at the end of the day this will remain a pious hope until our law makers fully grasp the difference in the psychology of social behaviour in the rural and urban set up. The elite thinkers must condescend to engage in subaltern studies to know more of the impending challenges to social order in our very times.

9

Dr. Sahib Singh Verma: Powerhouse on the Move

It was the late afternoon of 2nd July. As I drove past Najafgarh through the rugged road across small villages to reach where the mortal remains of Dr. Sahib Singh Verma were to be consigned to the sacred fire, stirring thoughts crossed my mind. I had gone through a similar experience earlier in the morning at 5 at Tughlak Lane standing stunned like many others big and small who had thronged the place to pay their homage to the departed soul.

As the flower bedecked the cottage carrying the mortal remains of Dr. Sahib Singh Verma slowly hurtled through the drive way among the wailing of ladies of the family and others who had gathered to mourn mixed with slogans of 'Dr. Sahib Singh Verma Amar Rahe and Jab Tak Suraj-chand Rahega Verma ji ka Naam Rahega' renting the air. It was a heart rending moment indeed and a moment for the mind to take charge for controlling the swelling emotions before they streamed out through the eyes.

My chain of thoughts was broken as my vehicle converged on Rohtak Road where a policeman on duty guided me to a place for parking my car. A few kilometres stretch of Rohtak Road, National Highway No.10 passing by the site marked for cremation had been closed for general Traffic. Large crowds had already gathered at the venue converging from all directions from the city, its suburbs, the towns and from village far and near and of course almost every one from the native village Mundka of Dr. Sahib Singh Verma. They were all there to have a last glimpse of the son of the soil whose reputation had remained unsoiled in the murky world of politics.

Politicians and public men of all hues transcending artificial boundaries, impelled by the feeling of personal bonds which Dr. Verma had built all along his life had come to pay their tribute to their Sahib. As the pallbearers entered the arena of the proposed Sports School, the otherwise disciplined crowds jostled to find vantage points to witness the last rites. The Early birds had perched themselves on the high boundary walls of the complex not mindful of the hot sun.

With the VIP's having placed their wreathes, the customary last rites were performed amid chanting of *vedic* mantras. The crowd again echoed the slogans 'Dr. Sahib Singh Verma Amar Rahe And Jab Tak Suraj Chand Rahega.' The last moment arrived. The pyre decked with the mortal remains of Dr. Verma merging in the pure wood was lit with fire which would take it to the higher realms of heaven as per the *vedic mantra*: *om agne naya supatha raye asman vishwani deva vayunani vidwan! Yuyoddhyasmajjuhuranameno bhuyishtham te nama uktim vidhema!!*

Sahib Singh had gone for another tryst with his Sahib, to be in His service, intent to take up any role that may be awaiting him. For the present he has left images and memories of a spirited man dedicated to higher causes. I had known Dr. Sahib Singh Verma for the last over thirty years. He was a self-made man in profession, career and political life. By sheer dint of his hard work, devotion and sincerity of purpose, and above all by his clarity of mind he was able to carve out position of honour in public life.

His two separate stints as Minister and Chief Minister of Delhi and later as Cabinet Minister in the Central Government brought out the best in him. He rose to the Vice-President of Bharatiya Janata Party which he served as a true soldier, giving little quarter to be dissidence even when there could be legitimate grounds for grievance.

He had succeeded in politics. But he did not seem to see that as the end goal. It was a means for doing service to the people, especially people from the village and the poor everywhere. His involvement as a social worker was intense. He was especially adapt in running to the rescue of the poor & needy.

His Accessibility was a routine and his availability a legend. He did not turn down any one's invitation at social or other functions and did not fail to appear in response-an almost impossible feat which became a legend very early in his public life. He could be seen appearing at marriage functions no matter if it was at the last ceremony of *vida* and lending a helping hand to push the yet to be powered vehicle poised to carry the bride.

Whether it was a case of getting a poor patient released from a private hospital detained for want of payment of the bill or it was ensuring the admission of some needy student in a professional college without payment of capitation fee against a pledge of personal appearance at the functions of the college. He came out in a big way for funds for providing succour to the widows and orphans of the Kargil war. Equally praise worthy was his initiative in organizing the rehabilitation of poor people of Bhuj affected by earthquake.

I had the opportunity to personally see him at work on several occasions. I observed him as uniquely gifted with the capacity to take quick and correct decisions. His grass root connection stood him in good stead and he never snapped this connection. On becoming Minister in Delhi Government for the first time be had dropped at my residence in the University when my wife and I were away in Australia. On my return I Called him on telephone. He expressed his desire to call on me. I however, insisted to let that be my privilege first. He agreed and as decided I reached his office in the old Secretariat at 7:30 in the morning. While on my way I had wondered what Verma ji would be doing in his office at such and early hour in winter. As I found my way to his chamber through an alley crowded by visitors I was amazed to find a swarm of people mostly villagers occupying all the chairs available with many just hustling around. Verma ji was not in his chair and was going round and reaching out to each visitor individually, hearing their grievances and receiving representations.

Giving me a chair near his to sit in he continued his foray with the people. A little later he settled in his seat and got engaged in hearing complaints and offering solution to be noted by the officers assisting him. Having watched him patiently of sometime and having complimented him for his style of working, I expressed my desire to take leave of him. He immediately stood up and escorted me to the anteroom where he had already got arrangement made for breakfast I returned to my office admiring his simplicity and preparedness to get at the root of things before taking a decision while at the same time saving time over procedures.

As Education Minister Dr. Sahib Singh took initiatives in opening new colleges in Delhi, Aditi Mahavidyala in Bawana, Keshav Mahavidyala in Shakurpur, Bhaskaracharya College of Applied Sciences in Dwarka, Maharaja Agrasen College in Mayur Vihar and Maharshi Valmiki College of Education in Madhuvan are the Results of his efforts. He was almost always present to personally interact with the inspection Committees of the University of Delhi Which I as Dean of Colleges of the University, had the privilege of heading.

Both of us together geared our personal equation for the benefit of extending educational facilities in Delhi. Once I spoke to him about the shortage of space in Bhaskaracharya College, then functioning temporarily in a portion of the building of the ITI at Pusa. A day or two later Verma ji took me along in a meeting arranged by him at ITI Pusa to inspect their arrangements for the certificate course in Hotel Management. The meeting proved fruitful in the sense the problem got solved without any ado. The Principal of the ITI felt honoured by the Gesture of the Minister in Personally visiting his Institute. In Bonus we had the benefit of relishing the tasty dish *Kheer* in the hospitality department there.

But alas in spite of the positive efforts made by both of us and the cooperation extended by the Vice-Chancellor, the proposal of the Defence Authorities to open a college in Delhi Cantonment could not Materialize as the UGC did not accept the principle of reservation in admissions for the wards of Defence Personnel, Serving or Retired.

Of late, Dr. Verma had vastly enhanced his activities in the field of social work and was set to institutionalize the same. He believed in dictum of "*Charvaiveti, Charaiveti*" and led by example. He was always pulsating with energy which he harnessed through a life style, simple and subtle at the same time. He walked briskly and his strides were wide. He was a power house on the move. He would be remembered for years to come for all that he did and for all that he refrained from doing and would continue to inspire many a young mind. May God gives rest to his soul.

10

Vestiges of Vedic Culture Among the Jats

Fewer questions of Indian History have elicited bipolar answers than the question of the identity and origin of the people who are today known as or call themselves Jats. On the one hand there are die hard protagonists who would not move an inch from their stated position that the Jats are-none other than the inheritors and descendants of the indigenous Aryan people who millenniums ago traversed the land called *Saptasindhu* in the hymns of the Rig Veda. On the other hand we have scholars who are not prepared to accept the Jats even as indigenous people and clubbing them with their brethren, the Rajputs and Gujjars trace their origin in the invading Hunas and Shakas on the basis of some far-fetched similarity of some solitary custom or belief in utter disregard of yawning evidence permeating the daily life of the Jats strongly pointing to their Vedic connection. In an attempt to drive a wedge between the Rajputs and the Jats the famous historian of the Rajputs James Todd sought to establish the Vedic Aryan connection for the Rajputs putting the Jats in the category of foreign immigrants, though not denying the essential similarities between the two great castes. Among the protagonists we have distinguished foreign writers like H. Risley, Denzil Ibbetson, Dr. Trumpp and Beams etc. Grierson, faced with the strong evidence of linguistic content, grudgingly accepted the Aryan origin of the Jats but not before categorizing them as degraded Aryans. Indian writers tracing an Aryan origin of the Jats include scholars like Thakur Deshraj (*Jat Itihas*), G.S. Ghurye (*Castes and Tribes of India*), K.R. Qanungo (*History of Jats*), B.S. Dahiya (*Jats : the Ancient Rulers*), Hukani Singh Pawar (*The Jats, Their Origin, Antiquity and Migrations*) etc. though among themselves, they differ with regard to the indigenous home of the Aryans. Thakur Deshraj, and following him Hukam Singh Pawar connect the Jats with the Aryans via the Shaka route i.e. a branch of the Shakas was originally of vedic Aryan stock. This at best can be described as proxy for the Shaka origin of the Jats, which falls neither here nor there. B. S. Dahiya tracing a foreign origin of the Aryans themselves falls into the web of etymology and finds himself in an inextricable position in the absence of adequate tools of scientific and historical methodology.

A superficial view of the Jat way of life on the part of the scholarly world can be seen as a major road block in the way of tracing the vedic link of the Jats. As Qanungo points out, almost all observers generally agree that in religious and social usages the Jats do not differ much from other Hindu communities of admittedly Aryan origin. In fact the label Hindu or Indu was given to the inhabitants on both sides of the river Indus (Sindhu) by the Persian king Darius (522-486 B.C.) and by Xarxes (465 B.C.). The Greeks called the people of this region Indoi (from which the word Indian is derived). Rigveda is conversant with the river Sindh and its seven tributaries. The tract traversed by these seven rivers is called *Saptasindhu* in the Rigveda. The *Saptasindhu* region of the Vedas is known to have been inhabited by the Jats. So there is no reason to deny the Rigvedic connection of the Jats.

Let us examine a few features of the vedic culture reflected in the life of the Jats. Entering the religious domain we find a refreshing echo of the vedic religion in the beliefs and practices of the Jats all along the ages. The Rigvedic seer candidly declares–*ekam sad viprah bahudha vadanti* i.e. 'wise men describe (pray to) one Reality (God?) in many ways (or forms)'. The Jat has never been in doubt about oneness of God and formal worship of a particular deity has not been found to be his problem. It is not that he does not believe in worshipping God. He does. He can pray without uttering a single word of formal prayer. He is quite conscious of the essential unity of all souls but he does not believe in running after agents to get him religious merit. When he says-'what matters in life is action, and prayer in any form reaches God *(kar le so kam, bhaj le so Ram),* he is only echoing the Ishavasyopanishad which sings- '*Kurvanneveha karmni jijivishet shatam samah'-one* should continue to do one's duties and wish to live hundred years'. The Jat in the fashion of his Vedic ancestor is aware of the glories of the elements of nature. The rivers are sacred to him and he recognizes the value of water. He lives by and can die for water. The sacred Ganga is a swear word for him which he would not like to falsify at any cost. As a true householder he knows how to keep fire *(Agni)* going. The kind wind *(Vayu)* and the strong storm all visit his life and he takes all phenomena in their stride as God's doings. The sky (*Dyaus*) far above, blue in hue, is synonymous with formless (*nirakara*) God whom he calls *Ramji* (not to be confused with Shri Ram of the Ramayana). What the famous Earth (*Prithvi*) Hymn of the Atharvaveda (XII.1) contains by way of lessons on environmental protection and sustainable development *(sa no bhumi vardhayad vardhamana)*\ co-existence of different elements of a plural society, is eminently demonstrated in the life and beliefs of the Jat of yesterday and today in ample measure. The child and mother relationship of man with the Earth (*mala bhumi putro=ham prithivyah)* runs through the veins of every Jat, who tears the crust of the earth and in turn gets his food in the manner of from his mother. The agenda chartered by the Rig Veda for the simple peasant in the famous hymn of Gambler (X.34.13) has been scrupulously pursued by the Jat peasants for thousands of years. The Rig Veda *declared-akshair ma divyah, krishim it krishasva* i.e.' do not play with the dice, play a true ploughman.' The Jat has not failed to follow the dictum. In the words of Father Wendel, the pioneer historian of the Jats, 'to be Jat, is to be peasant or ploughman'.

The social life of the Jats (known by any name in the past) cast in the Vedic mould has hardly changed in its essentials except in cutting some corners. The familial relationship based on sound ethnological principles have remained personalized without getting faceless even with the ever growing dimensions of social change. Every one means something to everyone else here. The ideals of marriage set out in the Rigveda (X.85) in its Hymn of Marriage have been the guiding star for matrimony among Jats for the many past centuries. All marriages are performed overall *agnihoma* with the recitation of Vedic mantras. The components of the ceremony do not fail to include the vedic prayer for well-being; the mandatory oblations offered in the fire alter; the couple going round the fire alter holding hand (X.85.36,38); offering libations of parched rice in the fire alter; the bride touching a rock with her toe; sighting the pole star; filling with vermilion the parting of the hair of the bride by the groom, the father giving the hand of his daughter to the groom, and finally the couple walking seven steps together, each affirmed by a Vedic vow made public. Some of the post marriage ceremonies have a vedic origin. The age old custom of appearance of the bride *(munh dikhai*) before close relations and friends of the family is based on the Rigvedic (X. 85.33) *mantra-'sumangaliryam vadhurimam Sameta pashyata, saubhagyam asyai datvayathastam vipratana* i.e. here is this bride of auspicious men, come all, see her face and then having showered her with blessings, return. The bride is welcomed in her new home with the same fanfare as contemplated in the Rig Veda. The vedic wish for the bride to have place of honour in her in-laws' house have not remained mere pious words among the Jats. Elderly ladies of the community showering blessing on a bride are seen wishing her begotten sons and grandsons remind us of the Rigvedic (X.85.18,19) tradition. If a Jat craves for a son he only betrays a vedic belief where–sonlessness was–as much deplored as–poverty (Rigveda, III.16.5). Again his moorings are traceable to the Rigveda (VII.4.7,8) when we find him not opposing adoption but hardly resorting to it. Probably it had something to do with custom of restricting ownership of land to the members of the *gotra* of the same village, which system if adopted would result in alienation of land to person of other *gotras*. However under the dispensation of the modern State things have changed radically, though not fully. The practices of endogamy of caste and exogamy of *gotra* prevalent among the Jats for ages is a faithful representation of the prohibitions in relation to matrimony prescribed by the *Dharmasūtra*s and the *Smritis*, viz. *sagotra, sapravara, sapinda and viruddha- sambandha.*

The *Brahmana* finds a place of respect in the scheme of things of the Jats. It is well known that the *Brahmana* has enjoyed a respectable and privileged position in society for his role as the repository and propagator of the ancient wisdom contained in the Vedas as also the priest par excellence for all religious ceremonies. Among the Jats, who are not very concerned about the formalism of rituals the *Brahmana* commands respect more for his intellectual attainments in accordance with the standard set forth in the Atharva Veda (V.19.8) Viz. '*Brahmanam yatra hinsanti tad rashtram hanti duchchhuna*' i.e. 'that smites the kingdom, where they do harm to any intellectual'. The Jats show respect to every *Brahmana* addressing every one as *dada* irrespective of age or relative hierarchy of a clan. The legendary hospitality of the Jats has connection with the vedic psyche of invoking *Agni*, the most important deity of the Rigveda with The epithet of 'guest' most frequently.

There is repeated mention of the democratic Bodies like *Sabha, Samiti* and *Vidatha* in the Vedic literature as fora for discussion and decision making on matters of public interest. The word *panchajana* or *panchamanava* also occurs quite frequently indicating some kind of local *panchayat* system working in the vedic age. The *khap* and *sarvakhap* system of the Jats at the micro and macro level respectively is known to have guided the affairs of the society for ages and is not known to be defunct even today in spite of the alternative *panchayats* recognized and regulated by the government concerned, and we find it rising to the occasion on questions of crucial social content. The records kept of these informal *panchayats* bear out the continuity among the Jats of the Vedic traditions for centuries. It is a pity that such *panchayats* become active only sporadically as the initiative has been appropriated by the power of the state which in turn has its own credentials formed as it is on the strength of public support in elections. The Jat tradition of not including their females in the customary *panchayat* conventions can be traced back to its roots in the Atharvaveda (VII.39.4) where the house wife tells her husband, 'Here (at home) I shall speak, and you shall not. You can speak in the Assembly'. Who would deny that even though customarily the females did not enter the *panchayat* arena their views did hot remain unrepresented? Are we not entitled to argue the same way in the context of the demand of reservation for women in the representative Bodies above the *panchayats* in rural areas and Municipal Bodies in urban areas of our country?

And last but not the least we can't fail to notice the flavour of Vedic Sanskrit in their spoken tougue–the *Khadi Boli,* the immediate mother of the standard Hindi, our national language today. The nomenclatures of their traditional tools, food and drinks, clothes and ornaments, the flora and fauna that abound their tract, and above all their simple and carefree life style have Vedic aroma.

To conclude we may say that the Jats in their sedentary life style have preserved several elements of Vedic life even with the passage of thousands of years and say conversely that the Jats represent the best specimen of the Vedic Aryans.

11

Dealing with the Disconnect

The last century witnessed the spread of education of the western model in India. While the British India Government on its part opened universities and schools and colleges to prepare manpower to Indianise their administration, particularly at the lower echelons, caste groups came forward as entrepreneurs in the field with a view to be at the helm of educational management, looking therein an opportunity to benefit their own caste men (and women?). The latter had already before them a model in the trend of vociferous caste groups opening co-operative banks, community centres, hospitals and *Dharmaśālā*s intended for use of their caste group. However, the nationalistic spirit kindled by the freedom struggle under the leadership of Mahatma Gandhi seemed to have overtaken the fissiparous tendencies, and the early years of independent India gave currency to the Nehruvian slogan 'unity in diversity', the partition of India on religious grounds notwithstanding. Very soon the system of spoils of office falling into a few hands resulted in the multitudes getting reduced to the margins. Unity came under strain, at times grave one. The reorganization of states on linguistic grounds was not a linguistic issue alone. Ethnicity coinciding with commonality of language had a lot to do with it. Simultaneously we witnessed the phenomenal increase in the number of self- financing private institutions in technical and professional higher education, especially in the south and western regions of our country. North and north western parts remained almost insulated from such ventures, firstly for the reasons of state policy, and secondly due to lack of private initiative.

Delhi region inhabited by educationally deprived farmers, peasants and other workers presented a unique picture of contradictions. While on the one hand it boasted of a couple of renowned central universities and number of prestigious colleges in addition to other specialized institutions, it was abounding in large multitudes of youth either not reaching the level of college education or not being able to get admission to a relevant course as the educational institutions here, being part of a central university drew students from all parts of the country leading to fierce competition. A Study made some years back had shown, the Jawaharlal Nehru University did not have on its rolls a single student from the village Munirka on whose land the University is housed. Nevertheless, managing higher education had continued to be seen as a matter of prestige for a community for many reasons. The example of a couple of business houses and other groups running colleges in Delhi has over the years demonstrated the extent of patronage they commanded.

It was in this back ground that some socially spirited individuals among the Jats of Delhi mooted the idea of establishing a college in Delhi in the name of Maharaja Surajmal of Bharatpur and with the blessings of the then Maharaja Brijendra Singh of Bharatpur got the Surajmal (in those days people were shy of using the word Maharaja or the word Jat) Memorial Education Society registered under the Societies Registration Act of 1860 in 1972 as the first step towards the goal. Coincidentally one of the members of the group Dr. Balbir Singh was teaching at one of the colleges of Delhi University and his former teacher Dr. Sarup Singh happened to be the Vice-Chancellor of the University at that time. One can't say if the move was inspired by this fact. The group referred to above one day met Dr. Sarup Singh to seek his blessings (or help) for the proposed venture. There was nothing wrong or improper in the move. It was perhaps a bid to deal with the rural urban disconnect in the realm of education. There was already the example of the Ahir community with the initiative of Rao Birendra Singh having opened Rao Tula Ram College in Delhi University. It is different matter that it went defunct not long after its birth. Dr. Sarup Singh, having had first-hand experience with regard to the uncertain fate of the managements of colleges run by different caste communities, gave sane counsel to the group advising them not to go for a replicating college under the University of Delhi but to work towards the establishment of an institution with relevant courses where they could retain the initiative that had fired their imagination.

The advice was well taken. The group returned with a resolve to work incessantly towards such a goal. After years of hard work and extensive leg work by a devoted band of pioneers the Society swelled in number of members. With help and support from several resourceful members and other well- wishers the Society got from the DDA about eight acres of Land in Janakpuri in 1976. The hitherto nebulous idea of an educational institution started showing contours of shape of things to come after the issue had been discussed over several sessions of the meetings of the Society's active members, under the inspiring and able guidance of Shri Nathu Ram Mirdha and Shri Ram Niwas Mirdha. The first phase of the building programme was launched on 14 December 1978 with the then President of India Shri Neelam Sanjiv Reddy laying the foundation Stone in the presence of Chaudhary Charan Singh. In a couple of years the building having been ready certificate and diploma level courses in engineering and pharmacy were started.' The Delhi government agreed to allow the advantage of 15 percent in marks in case of students having not less than four years of schooling in rural areas. This measure went a long way in ensuring the admission of a good number of students from the villages. A new block of building and a four storey hostel was soon put in place. Things looked bright. But unfortunately the benefit of rural schooling having been withdrawn a couple of years later, fees not being revised, the salary bill of the staff going up year after year with the increase in DA, poor quality of students admitted through the centralized system, declining status of discipline etc. sounded an alarm. The situation left no option with the management but to close the admissions for future. But the remedy brought in other problems. The salary bill continued to be paid. Source of income (fees) dried. Some members of the staff went to court against the closure of admissions. There was a crisis. The Head of the Institution was clueless of the way out and could not do much apart from watching the spectacle of events. Many among the teachers being idle went about politicking and playing blame games which brought no repute to the Society. A serious disconnect had occurred.

With fresh thinking by the management in 1998-99 things started changing for the better. Admissions to diploma courses were revived. Degree courses in BBA, BCA and B.Ed. were started under a new Institute viz. Maharaja Surajmal Institute (1999). It was followed by the starting of Maharaja Surajmal Institute of Technology (2001) and Maharaja Surajmal Institute of Pharmacy (2003). Study Center of the Indira Gandhi National Open University was opened which brought the much needed recurring extra revenue. Construction of more buildings was taken up and completed speedily, the latest being the state of the art air- conditioned auditorium. Several new courses were added and seats increased. Placement of students was given priority. Amazing targets were achieved and the results showed the high academic level of the three Institutes. All round progress followed. The disconnect was handled wisely ensuring good health of the Society.

Where do we go from here? Higher, and higher no doubt, but not without the vision getting broader day by day and not without dealing with the disconnect which could occur in the working of any democratically managed organisation aspiring to reach pinnacles of glory. Surely, taking policy decisions, creating infrastructure, recruiting staff and general supervision are the normal[1] functions and responsibility of the management. The day to day running of the Institutes should logically be the responsibility of the respective Director and his colleagues.

It is here that disconnect can occur if one fails to work harmoniously for the realization of a vision. If we recruit Directors from among members of your own community we may undervalue them or alternatively they may outsmart everyone by hobnobbing with and politicking among the members of the management or conversely they may become victims of some elements in the staff hobnobbing with the management. In either case the result is indiscipline. The result is the same if the management entertains or encourages any member of the staff to reach them directly to give information (misinformation?) about affairs of the Institute concerned with the motive of seeking unearned favours. Situations of the management having less reliance on the Director can lead to serious disconnect. As past experience has shown Politicking on the part of the members of the staff on the one hand and the Director on the other tacitly or inadvertently inspired by any member of the management is a sure prescription for ill health of the Institution.

Problems of management arising in any Institute should be sorted out with the respective Director across the table informally, rather than making it an issue on formal forum for scoring points. Observing protocol at all levels would go a long way in solving problems and maintaining congeniality. The functions of the management should very rarely touch the academic domain. The Directors on their part should have regular briefing de-briefing sessions with the Chairman or his nominee's and not leave issues accumulating closer to their chest or pending till the holding of formal meetings of the Governing Body. All persons working under instruction and on behalf of the Chairman have to keep in mind the dignity and persona of the Chairman. Sensitivity of an issue should be matched by the level of response.

As per the Memoranda of Association the Society's membership is open to all citizens of India irrespective of their caste creed or religion and the Society is apolitical in nature. But there is a disconnect. In practice membership of the Society is restricted to members of our community, with the exception of a very microscopic number of members from other communities. At the earlier stages of membership campaigns, its representatives went about focusing on the caste character of the Society for obvious reasons. It is expected therefore that some members, at various fora, especially on the occasion of the General-Body meeting, every year tend to set and reset the agenda for the Society. If the Society were to take up exterior (to its stated objectives) agenda there would be an overlap/ conflict with the already active several organisations operating in the name of the community of Jats viz. the Jat *Sabhas* and societies under different names of various colours and persuasions. Many members of these Societies are parallel members of our Society.

Sometimes members adhering allegiance to other societies also have been seen making attempt to realise the aspirations of those societies on the platform of our Society. The working President of one such society speaking at a joint social function held at our Society/premises did not find it inappropriate to announce a certain policy initiative, that the host Society should take, embarrassing himself and others in the process. With the Surajmal Memorial Education Society, gaining more and more heights year after year this trend has become quite common. No wonder then that the ' Society is attracting the covetous eyes of some politicians looking for a chance to keep afloat in prominence by being at its helm directly or through proxy. They would not consider the stark contrast they present in front of the eminence and probity of the present Chairman who has given much to the Society instead of taking any thing from it. But happily vast majority of members understand things and ensure that such attempts are *ab initio* thwarted.

Things also get a bit complex when persons of proven integrity and dynamism working as important functionaries of our society are sucked into assuming key positions in other organisations solely of our community (good people are needed every where). Positioning themselves on both sides of the dividing line it often becomes difficult for them to notice the 'No Man's Land' and the borderlines between Societies start getting blurred, innocently though, to the chagrin of the members with singular loyalty on either side. It is therefore more important for such functionaries in the management of the Society that they choose their preferences and priorities rather judiciously. Encumbrances created at one end, if carried over to another forum can sometimes lead to avoidable situations. It has happened a couple of years ago in an organization of our community, resulting in the expulsion of a key functionary reportedly on grounds, including financial irregularity. It also happened to be a case of dual loyalty. The same gentleman is facing contempt proceedings in a court of law for indulging in vilification campaign against the very Society to which he claims to have rendered yeoman's services and still holds its membership. Instead of restraining himself from such activities he has chosen to continue with these. One can only hope that this gentleman would see reason some day.

Then there is the need for reconciling the disconnect between the objectives of the Society in respect of our three Institutions and the unstated objectives sought to be achieved in the over all frame work of law. It is not disputed that as long as the norms of affiliation are adhered to there should be normally no restriction on the Society carrying out activities on the campus extraneous to the activities of the Institutions, both academic and others. In fact, some of them could be combined and integrated for creating needed synergy. The programmes and activities of the Research and Publication Centre, especially the feature of annual seminars eminently fall in this category. But we have to be vary of any excessive dose of activities which are of little interest to the students at large and are not of academic nature could only contribute towards the alienation of a vast section of them which might go to affect the over all image of the Society as an educational stakeholder, competing in the world of self financing institutions. So a fine balancing act is required on our part in this respect.

It is much often demanded from the platform of the Society by several well meaning but less knowledgeable persons that students from our own community should be given priority in admissions to the courses being run in our three Institutions. It should be known that the affiliation rules nowhere except in the case of minority institutions permit admissions on the ground of caste, creed or religion alone irrespective of what the commitments or ideology of any management are. Even then all efforts are made to accommodate students from our community against management quota seats within the framework of Government and University norms. It is seldom realized in many quarters that the non denial of employment opportunities to deserving persons from our community both in the teaching and non teaching staff by our management is a considerably positive out come of managing institutions of higher education, a field where our young and deserving men and women find it hard even to get entry elsewhere to prove themselves. And the bonus is in the form of opportunity to utilize the surplus, arising from prudent financial management, for taking up new projects, for furthering the cause of education, especially by taking it to the doorsteps of the rural people to whom the Society owes not little.

Last but not the least is the disconnect between the provision of the management quota in admissions to various courses and the stringent logistics prescribed for managing it. The provision raises high expectations among the public at large and the members of our own community in particular. It is almost impossible task for the management to reconcile the two. There are many red faces during admissions each year. It becomes difficult to convince many that there are constraints in filling management seats too. Functionaries working on behalf of the management in this exercise, indeed perform almost yogic feats. In fact all disconnects offer opportunities for assuming such postures for healthy results.

12

Kinship and Family in Kautilya

Family is the basic and universal structure of human society. Everywhere in all peasant societies there has been a predominance of extended families. Such societies are generally-as can be said of major parts of India since early times–patrilocal and patriarchal. There women find themselves in a relatively subordinated position brought about by the circumstance of their dependency on males of the family representing physical power so vital for carrying out the responsibilities of the occupation. Interpersonal relations of all members are authoritarian based on the myth of male superiority. Marriage is governed by kinship rather than by courtship and considered an interfamilial concern and not in interpersonal concern. Personal freedom, especially of the female is foreign to this life. Where knowledge-largely confined to vocations- is transmitted orally hierarchy of age determined relative authority. The above paradigm can be said to be true in the case of the society of early feudalism that developed in India in the post vedic period-a period which witnessed great churning in terms of social, political, cultural and philosophical ideas. India was, for the first time, attacked by a foreign power-the Macedonian conqueror, Alexander the great. It was the time when the largely fragmented land was occupied by many small monarchical principalities and numerous self sufficient republics. A major happening took place when aided by the giant strategist Chanakya Chandragupta established the great Mauryan empire putting together extensive areas from the Gangetic Valley to the Indus valley after dethroning the nasty Nanda dynasty.

Chanakya, by another name Kautilya is reputed to have authored the highly secular work *Arthaśāstra* to serve as an ideal compendium on statecraft which has not forgotten to emphasise welfare of the people as the key word for the ultimate success of a ruler. We may here recall the relevant stanza from the *Arthaṣāstra* (1.19.34) :

Prajasukhe sukham rajnah prajanam cha hite hitam
Natmapriyam hitam rajnah prajanam tu priyam hitam

[In the happiness of his subjects lies the king's happiness; in the welfare of the subjects lies his welfare. The king should not consider good only that which pleases him but treat as beneficial to him whatever pleases his subjects.]

It is in this context of welfare that Kautilya scores by giving his own tinge of safeguards for members of the weaker sex in whatever station he finds them. It was not in his hands or of the organized imperial state, whose interests he was promoting, to make a substantial dent in the established social order so strongly built and nurtured by the monolithic Brahmanic literature. But it must go to his credit that he recognized the realities of the situation and did his best to resurrect the position of women. We, may here gainfully examine his general approach in societal matters in the limited sphere of family and kinship.

It cannot be said with an amount of certainty whether the *Kautilyan family* was extended, joint, nuclear or conjugal but we can glean from his work a fair picture of the nature of relationships and personal rights and duties of the different members of the family as also the related rules and procedures including those concerning inheritance succession and partition of wealth and property. However, we learn that there were families which had the following members; the father or the *grihapati;* presumably his mother; the *grihapati* himself, his wife or wives; his brother/s and sister/s; his son/s; his daughter/s; grandson/s and presumably grand-daughters. Possibility of the family patriarch living till he had great grand-children cannot be ruled out as Kautilya talks of dividing the hitherto un-partitioned property among the scions up to four generations (3.5.4, *Kangle's* Vol. II, p. 209). Doubt with regard to properties lying un-partitioned for several generations are not unknown among some agricultural communities of North

India especially the Jats. Till the middle of the last century there were any number of extended families living together with common land holding. No doubt, this phenomena is throwing up problems of its own sort when joint family system has long lost its sway.

Family represents the second stage i.e., *grihastha,* a house holder's life in a man's life in the scheme of the four *Dharamas.* It is an important stage when one contributes to economic activity and maintenance of social order in perpetuating the family line. Kalidasa calls this stage the *sarvabhogya ashrama* (stage of life, sustaining all). To talk about family one has to go back to its basis i.e., marriage and the attending parameters. Kautilya declares that the aim of taking a wife is to beget sons (I think also daughters)- *putrartha hi striyah* (3.2.42). Manu (9.26) says the same and a little more in the following words:

Prajanartham mahahhagah pujarha grihadiptayah
Striyah sriyashcha geheshu na visheshosti kashchana

In fact according to Kautilya man enters civil life with marriage- *avivahad vyavaharah* (3.2.1).

Though refreshingly radical and progressive thinker, Kautilya does not proceed to demolish the established cultural paradigms. He not only recognizes the *Varna* System and the traditional eight forms of marriage but also innovates in categorising the four of them as *dharmya* without pronoucing the rest four by any label like *adharmya* or the like. He is for *Varna* vise endogamic marriages but fully recognizes situations where this rule would be transgressed and therefore, accordingly apportions the relative status to the progeny resulting from such marriages.

Father being the head of the family takes most decisions but there are situations when the mother also figures in decision making. The first four of the eight forms of marriage are lawful with the sanction of the father, the remaining four with the sanction of the father and the mother, both (3.2.11).

Kautilya was fully aware of the vulnerability of women before and after marriage. He therefore proceeds to provides safeguards within the prevailing social ethos and brings in the role of the state in prescribing punishment, mostly in the form of fines, for violations of the relevant law. It also served as a means of more revenue to the state. Some of his provisions appear to be ahead of the modern day concerns of the lawmakers. Thus we have Kautilya forestalling present day feminists when he expects the husband to treat the newly wed lady with utmost civility in teaching modest behaviour and not to use abusive expressions like *'nashte'* (you are lost [beyond redemption]; *'vinashte'* (you are thoroughly ruined); *'nyange'* (you are a cripple); *'apitrike'* (you do not know who your father was); *'amatrike'* (your mother abandoned you) [3.3.7]. However, (in case of a slow learner?) a mild strike on the back with either a split bamboo cane or a rope or hand is permitted By making the breach of the above rule a punishable offence he leaves no scope for platitudes, an area where male chauvinists of our times are past masters.

Polygamy was not unknown to Kautilya. However, he was, aware of the insecurity this practice could bring about for the existing wife. He therefore provides safeguard, at least economic by making it obligatory for the husband to pay to the wife the dowry amount, the woman's property and in the case of a wife without a dowry or woman's property of her own a compensation for supercession equal in amount to that, and a suitable maintenance. (3.2.41). Kautilya would not like a* polygamous husband to neglect his conjugal obligations to any of his wives and therefore, he prescribes a detailed protocol for the purpose of conjugal relations (3.2.43-47). Breach of the rules makes the husband liable to a fine of maximum of twenty four *panas* (3.2.40).

Kautilya, to begin with states that there is no *divorce* in pious *(dharmya)* marriages (3.3.19). In other forms of marriage divorce is permissible with mutual consent (3.3.17). It is refreshing to note that Kautilya allows breaking of a marriage and abandonment of the husband by the wife if he has become degraded; is away from home for long time in a foreign land; is a traitor to the king; is dangerous to her life; is declared outcast; becomes impotent (3.2.48).

Kautilya does not see conjugal rights of the husband and the wife in isolation. While ensuring the realization of the respective rights of the two he takes note of situations where exceptions have to be made (3.2.45-47). He does a fine balancing act in dealing with the phenomenon of incompatibility of couples. A wife having dislike of her husband would permit him to go his own way to another woman (3.3.12). But a wife neglected by her husband was entitled to separate from him and live under the protection of a guardian, kinsmen or a mendicant woman (3.3.13). An unscrupulous husband falsely accusing an innocent wife in this respect is sought to be punished in place of being allowed to have his evil ways (3.3.14).

Physical virginity on the part of young girls before marriage and fidelity in marriage is of great importance for Kautilya. Having laid down the age of majority of twelve years for girls and sixteen years for boys, he would not like the young people to wait endlessly before embarking on their married life. How close we find it to the thinking of the Law commission reported in the media recently! He puts the onus on a father to marry off his daughter within three years of her attaining puberty failing which she was free to marry a man of the same *Varna* or even of a different *Varna,* forfeiting in the latter case the ornaments given to her by her father (4.12.10). She would be charged of theft if she took away her father's property, a disincentive for those planning elopement.

We find Kautilya quite stern in the matter of adulterous relationship. If the wife misbehaves when the husband is away on journey, the kinsman or his servant should put her under guard till her husband returns (4.12.30,31). If the husband tolerates, the wife as also the person committing the crime are set free (4.12.32), otherwise the wife shall be punished by cutting off of her ears and nose, the paramour meeting with death(4.12.33)-exemplary punishment indeed! But this does not imply that Kautilya was not aware of the basic right of the wife to have her conjugal life. He provides for remarriage of a woman in case of long absence of her husband or his becoming a mendicant after the prescribed period of wait of seven months to one year (where she has borne children (3.4.37). But the fiat is that the remarriage must be contracted with one among the kinsmen of the husband in a set order of preference (3.4.38-41). A woman marrying outside the prescribed list of heirs of the husband violating the kinship boundaries she, along with the man marrying her, will be punished for adultery (3.4.42). Even the accomplish would be similarly punished.

A wife is provided sufficient economic security right from the day of her marriage. Her property *(stridhana)* consists of an amount for her support and her jewellery. The amount of support would be an endowment of more than two thousand *panas*. There is no limit to the amount of jewellery (3.2.14,15). The wife was entitled to use her property for maintaining herself and her sons and daughters-in-law in case the husband makes no provision for maintenance of the family before going on long journey. A husband could use his wife's property for the performance of religious acts and to meet emergencies such as disease, famine and unforeseen dangers. The couple together could use it by mutual consent if they beget a son and a daughter (3.2.16). If the husband has had the use of his wife's property for three years the wife's right lasts in varying degree only in the last four types of marriage, her claim not sustaining in the first four types (3.2.17-18). This is in consensus with the virtual contractual nature of marriage in the last four types. In case of the wife predeceasing her husband her property shall be divided as under: sons and daughters in equal shares; daughters in equal shares if there were no sons; the husband if there are no children; the dowry, the marriage gifts and any other given by kinsmen shall be repatriated to the donors (3.2.36, 37). Quite an unusual provision indeed! A widow, not intending to remarry gets the support endowment, her jewellery, the balance of dowry if any and whatever was given to her by her husband during his lifetime (3.2.19). Even if she remarries, but with the approval of her father-in-law, she will receive what was given to her by her father-in-law and her late husband (3.2.21). On the death of the widow her property will pass on to her sons and daughters.

In the matter of inheritance and partition of ancestral property Kautilya follows the traditional Hindu practice as given in the *Dharmaṣāstras*. The basic principle is that sons inherit as the son performs ritual funeral and annual *pinda* ceremonies of his ancestors up to three previous generations-father, grand-father and great grand-father. Among the sons, the eldest bears the primary responsibility and is therefore entitled to a special share of the ancestral property. From among the twelve types of sons the *Aurasa* gets precedence. The categories of sonship are: *1. Aurasa; 2. Putrikaputra; 3. Kshetraja; 4. Gudhaja; 5. Apaviddha; 6. Kanina; 7. Sahoda; 8. Paunarbhava; 9. Datta; 10. Upagata; 11. Krtaka; 12. Krita.* The apportioning of shares in a partition in inheritance there is an elaborate procedure settling questions of seniority in age and status derived from the circumstance of marriage of the parents, premarital *Varna* of the respective parent (3.6.21). Though Kautilya has not said in so many words but it would be logical to assume inclusion of daughters in the various categories of sons stated by Kautilya because it is unthinkable that only sons were born in the situations described by him for the purpose of sonships. Lest this piece should turn into a listless catalogue let me conclude by saying that Kautilya had placed himself in the role of a social and political thinker committed to the establishment and consolidation of the imperial Mauryan state. In the process he had to deal with heterogeneous social norms and practices, disparate political arrangements with cultural and ethnic diversities. For bringing such a spectrum administratively under one umbrella he had to do lot of social engineering and political wire pulling. With regard to his relevance in our times one can only say that the nature of human beings remains the same. States behave the same way as they always have done. His details on battle formations and code of penalties may sound outmoded and simply having historical interest. But he is as topical as any modern expert when he discusses issues of economy, just administration, inter-state relations, intelligence gathering and espionage. We can learn a lot from him.

13

When Marriages Meant Merriment

Modernity while ameliorating many a hardship of life in rural India has taken a toll of many aspects of traditional ways of the people. Celebration of marriages particularly in rural areas has undergone a sea change. The old world charm of merrymaking and community participation has been overshadowed and rudely replaced by the loud and impersonal electronic media leaving only a passive role even for the main players and throwing community participation away from the main scene. Till the middle of the last century all that was old was gold. It may be worthwhile to recall the marriage scene of the old era for the benefit of our city sucked new generation of young folks with roots in villages. The post-harvesting season extending from May to July was generally preferred for solemnising marriages. The betrothal (*sagai*) ceremony preceding marriages by about a year's time used to be a simple affair but made impressive by the presence of the village elders and relatives and friends of the prospective groom. All present earned the sweets in the form of five *batashas* (small cakes of sugar) each and also a one rupee coin as a token of respect. But before deciding to go for the relationship it was ascertained that the prohibitions of not marrying inside the three *gotras* (viz. that of the father, the mother's father and the father's mother's father) were complied with. In the nineteenth century the mother's mother's father's *gotra* also fell in the prohibited category but had been dropped with the passage of time though no *khap panchayat* is believed to have sanctioned the practice. In the same way in the new third millennium in several places the *gotra* of the father's mother's father also has been taken out of the list at many places.

The date of marriage was fixed with mutual consultations of the two families and confirmed by the girl's parents through a letter called the *peeli chitthi* sent sufficiently in advance of normally four to five weeks followed by another similar letter called *lagna* some eleven days in advance of the date of marriage whereas at the bride's place the period ranged from five to seven days, invariably two days less than that in the former's case. This was called the period of *baans* during which the extended families and friends offered hospitality by treating to lunch all the members of the groom's and the bride's family as the case may be, including guests if any at their respective places. It meant no cooking at lunch time for the concerned family - a substantial relief in summer, especially when the guests started arriving several days in advance of the date of marriage. On the other hand the increased manpower helped in taking care of the additional work relating to the preparations for the marriage - community solution to individual problems! During this period the bridegroom and the bride got the treatment generally extended to very important persons. Both at their respective places were put to a daily regimen of application of paste made by mixing gram flour with turmeric *(ubtan/batna)* and mustard oil followed by a bath amid a ritual accompanied with singing of traditional songs by the women folk of the family and the neighbourhood. All this was geared to give a sense of well-being and physical fitness to the young couple to-be. The application of *ubtan* was supposed to enhance the fairness of the skin, an indication of the preference for a partner of fair colour. Amulets were tied on the wrist and the ankle of the groom and the bride to serve as marks of distinction and impending bonding and also signifying the medicinal efficacy of the contents ingrained in the amulets. The bridegroom, in addition carried an iron rod (*gaj*) shaped into a fancy walking stick with a tingling ring trapped at the lower end, supposedly to ward off evil. But I suppose it was meant to serve as a handy weapon in case of any emergency, say against a menacing dog or something.

Feast Flavour

The penultimate day was a day of community feast at the house of the bridegroom. The number of invitees depended on the social connections of the grooms family. However, beyond a limit the feast was no free lunch as the system of *nyolu nithar* (reciprocal contribution in cash) was in place. Under this system which still continues, financial contributions were made by the invitees on a calibrated basis to be recorded for future reciprocation. The details of receipts and payments on this account were kept in a special type of long folded book with a red cover called *bahi* and inscribed in the *Mundi* or *Modi* script by the village *mahajan* (trader). There was no confusion regarding the number of barber (*Nai*) who acted as the go-between and messenger at all stages of the marriage ceremony. He faithfully carried out the instructions regarding invitations specifying the number of persons to be invited from a family. As a general rule in most cases only one child accompanied an elder of the family clasping the latter's index finger. No objection was made to the additional member. Self-imposed discipline in such matters was taken for granted. Sometimes a niggardly host would make a physical check to ensure the adherence to the number expected at the feast. There were also some liberal hosts who left everything to the skies oblivious of any pilferage taking place under their nose with the connivance of the very persons who had been marshalled to protect his interest. The feasts comprised a very simple menu. At the bridegroom's place the main dish was *laddoos* (sweet balls) followed by *puries* served with some vegetable, usually of pumpkin. At the bridegroom's place *zalebi* was an additional dish. With the access to cities becoming easier more delectable dishes started appearing at the marriage feasts. Counts (like *satpakwani* etc.) done of the items served gave an idea of the level of the celebrations. But progressively the difference between menus served in marriage feasts in the villages and the cities or towns has gradually disappeared.

On the Mark

The march of the marriage party was preceded by the important ceremony of *Ghurcharhi.* The bridegroom mounting a mare followed by a procession of singing womenfolk went round the village, stopping at a temple or *Bhumia* seeking blessings and good luck. A musical band was in attendance playing contemporary tunes, provoking some young friends of the bridegroom to break into impromptu dancing. The marriage party, aiming to reach the bride's place early on the day of marriage, invariably started the journey the previous night. The Procession formed a caravan of bullock carts - large and small. Occasionally a horseman or two joined the party. At the centre stage used to be the decorated chariot *(ratha)* of the bridegroom having two compartments - one meant for the bride and her attendant and the other for the groom. The driver of the vehicle had a separate seat ahead. Such vehicles were not common. They were kept by selected families and were hired out during the marriage season at good price. A medium level version of the chariot was the *majholi* or *bahli* having only one compartment and with a lower height than that of the *ratha*. Merry making and fun and frolic continued throughout the journey. The occasion also witnessed some kind of competition in cart racing along mostly *kachcha* tracks. The winner earned a prize in the form of sweets. As marriages were generally solemnized during summer months, the members of the marriage party on arrival were offered *thandai* (a cold drink concocted by mixing paste of several ingredients including dry fruits and sugar in iced water). The bullocks yoked in the vehicles of the marriage party and horses if any also, received due attention at the bride's place. Their owners got a scaled ration of grain and fodder for their maintenance and comfortable stay. A modest band formed an integral part of the marriage party. The member of the band invariably belonged to the chuhara caste. The band playing choicest tunes would accompany the marriage party at all outings at different ceremonies at the bride's place. The marriage party was housed in the village *chaupal* (an open door community hall also used for holding meetings of the village *panchayat*). However, some members voluntarily opted for staying with some relatives of their own in the village concerned. But they were kept amongst of all the events in the ceremonies of marriage and were supposed to join the same.

Several Ceremonies

The bridegroom accompanied by a contingent of the *baraties* was received at the door head of the house of the bride's father by an assembly of women where the elder married sister or sister-in-law of the bride performed the welcome ritual by doing *arata* (*arati*) of the bride groom. It was known by the name *barauthi* (*dvara-stha* i.e. a call at the door), marriage was solemnized during late afternoon *godhuli* - when the cattle came home raising dust through hoofs in their strides). The ceremony was *havan* centric, amid chanting of Vedic mantras irrespective of the denomination - *aryasamaji* or *sanatan* of the priest. *Agni Pradakshina* (toeing a rock), *dhruvadarshana* (sighting the pole star) and *saptapadi* (walking seven steps together) were essential parts of the ritual. The ritual progressed amid singing of songs of the occasion by the ladies of the side of the bride. Some of these songs contained content deriding the members of the groom's party. The latter no doubt enjoyed the stuff as it all was said in jest. With the abolition of child marriage *patara pher* (exchanging seats, taking the bride to the left of the groom) slowly came to be general rule serving as a replacement of the ceremony of *muklawa* or *gauna*. Immediately after the marriage ritual was over the bride and the groom were conducted to the inner quarters of the bride's house where impressions of their palms soaked in *mehndi* and *ghee* alternatively were put on a specially prepared panel on one of the walls of the house. This practice along with several others served as a symbol of proof of marriage and continues to be followed, though today we have more enduring and legal tools to be used as documents attesting a marriage. Custom has its own charm and flavour even if redundant today. The crown mounted on the turban of the bride groom was retained by the bride's family and hoisted (prominently on the wall of the main room of the house as if to announce to strangers visiting the house of the event of marriage of a daughter having taken place in the family and, no doubt, serving a constant assurance of her having got a partner to the young bride.

The next and final day was the day of relaxation and (preparation for journey back to home early next morning. Lunch on the second day was a decentralized affair. The marriage party broke into small groups, each to be feasted by a householder close to the family of the bride. The menu used to be simple though not without a rich dose of *ghee* (clarified butter) and *boora* (refined sugar). This arrangement gave some respite to the bride's family and somre financial cushion too. *Vida* (send off) ceremony was the major event in the afternoon. The bride's family offered gifts and cash to the groom and members of his family. The members of the marriage party (received a rupee each as token of respect. Gradually with the passage of time a brass tumbler was added. The bridegroom gradually graduated to the entitlement to a golden ring, a watch and a bicycle. If the above three items included the gifts the marriage was ranked as the best possible settlement. These days we witness cars and many more expensive gifts finding easy passage to the quarters of the groom. After all the pie of the cake of progress must be shared. The şide of the bride groom did not fail to play host on this occasion. Anybody present there having married in the *gotra*/village of the bride groom was offered rupee one as token of honour. Any son of the above was similarly treated. The ladies of such families were inseparately honoured by the bride groom going round the village accompanied by a couple of younger members of the marriage party during evening hours and in turn getting sumptuously feasted with sweet hot milk.

Another important ceremony was the contribution of *bhat* by the brother of the mother of the bride or bridegroom as the case may be. It included clothes for the bridegroom/bride, the respective mother and near relatives and also some cash meant to offset part of the expenditure incurred on the marriage. Cases of the brother of father's mother also contributing some cash as *badbhat* were not uncommon. Early morning hours, before daybreak next day was the time for the bride's departure for her new home. An elder of the groom's family came forward to receive on the front of his shirt the seal of recognition in the form of an impression of the *mehndi* dipped palm of the bride's mother proudly disregarding the consequence of his new shirt getting soiled. Sometimes innocent pranks were played on such occasions. The bridegroom received farewell gifts in the form of modest amounts from cash (*jawahari*) of the ladies of the bride's family. The amount thus collected was perhaps meant for the couple to meet any contingencies arising immediately after the marriage.

Emotional Moments

The send-off scene became poignant with almost everyone in the bride's family sobbing amid tears and the bride crying as if she was being carried to a sacrificial alter (aren't we familiar with unending stories of bride burning and wife beating and dowry deaths!). There are stories of even the groom sobbing amid tears at such occasions. The ladies, especially the young girls from the circle of friends of the bride would burst into tears to the singing of the familiar song - *Saathan chaalpadi her mere dab dab bhar aaye nain*-our friend is leaving us, my eyes are overwhelmed with tears. Which heart would not melt at the sight of display of such tender emotions! Even the legendry *sanyasi babaji* squatting on the outskirts of a village could not help violating the contract to control his emotions and shed ocean of tears on one such occasion regardless of the prize that was to be his otherwise. Even a rock would melt or the core of a stone would fall asunder at such poignant moments as Bhavabhuti, the great Sanskrit playwright has aptly said in one of his plays-*api grava roditi api dalati vajrasya hridayam.*

Members of the marriage party *(baratis)* on the other hand feeling proud and pampered, ready with their respective vehicles would start their journey back to home engaging in a sort of competition for reaching the groom's place first would use all their navigating skills for a win. The front runners, however, were from among those who came in the rank of a brother-in-law of the bride. The winner would come and sit at the feet of the bride and utter the words "my sister-in-law shall get a son and I earn two sweetmeat balls" *(Bhabi ne beta, manne do laddoo).* Such scenes are rare these days.

These days ceremonies are cut short. Two day's ceremonies are completed the same day. Perhaps fast and easy availability of means of transport are responsible for the change- whether for the better or the worse it is difficult to say.

Slow Assimilation

Arriving at her new home the bride got ceremonial welcome accompanied with household rituals indicating the importance that was attached to the new member of the family. All efforts were made to make her feel comfortable at her new home by organizing, some fun filled games. Feasts were organized in her honour by friends of the family. She was hardly left alone to think of her parents home and family. A youngster of her family or a maid (a female of the Barbar's family) accompanied her as a mate. In the days of child marriage the role of the maid was very crucial, especially in protecting the Virginity of the child-bride till she returned to her parents' home. Some member of the bride's family, usually a brother arrived the next day to take her back a day after, the induction in the new family was made through a gradual process of frequent visits to her parental home. In the child bride the ceremony of *muklawa* was in vogue. Till this ceremony was performed a married girl living in the family of her father continued to wear a specially designed scarf *(doriya),* which indicated her marital status and the fact that she was under protection of one more family-that of her in-laws. Her honour was sacred trust to the whole of the village community. Marriage was supposed to be consummated only after this ceremony. Till it happened the bride and the groom were-not-allowed to see each other intimately. By the time of this ceremony the bride as well as the groom acquired the appropriate age for cohabitation. The period between marriage and *muklawa* could therefore be described as the time of courtship in absentia and the time for fostering conjugal fidelity. *Muklawa* was followed by *Doosar* (second coming) when the newly wed bride brought the first and the major instalment of clothes and ornaments for herself and presents for her near relatives, both male and female. The bride groom's sister was entitled to pick up at will any of the garments from the box of clothes brought by the bride. Sometimes it became a Hobson's choice for an innocent sister-in-law. Elderly ladies of the house were always around to help in the matter. Women of the village, young and old were invited to come and see the bride and the ware that she had brought from her parental home. The visitors (only ladies) from all parts of the village came in small clusters singing songs as they wended their way through the village alleys leading to the house of the host. Some elderly ladies of the neighbourhood paid modest amounts as a token of having seen the face of the bride *(Munh dikhai).* The bride on her part would offer reciprocal amount as recipient of blessing from the touch of their feet (*Panh padai).* The visitors got a modest sweet meat or a handful of boiled gram as a token of thanks.

It should be said to the credit of our women folk that they have been instrumental in preserving and carrying on the customs and traditions of social, life through the centuries and millenniums. Mercifully the emerging sop operas of the small screen are lately focusing on the customs and ceremonies, especially those relating to marriage. If it helps in igniting once again the fun and frolic and merry making by active participation of our men and women in the villages, we would say our villages are haven of happiness during marriage time.

14

Kin Names: Indicators of Social Networking Among the Jats

Nomenclatures of Kins prevalent among the Jats (in the broader sense to include other similar castes) of North India for centuries demonstrate a distinctly marked Sanskritic connection thereby with their Vedic origins. The social organization reflected in the Vedic literature, especially the *Rigveda* speaking of the family, the clan (or the gotra) and the village can be observed intact in many of its features in the kin organization of the Jats.

Some scholars believe kinship to be the origin of the caste system among the Hindus in India. There are others who consider vocation or profession as the basis of caste distinctions without wholly denying the role of kinship for the development of caste.

For the present, we may study the kin names and examine their degrees indicating an individual's status in social hierarchy, both in vertical and horizontal relationship.

Broadly speaking the kin terms can be placed into two categories- (I) those used for blood relations and (II) those applied to affinal (through marriage) kins. Each of these categories has primary and derived as also composite kin terms.

The first category goes three generation upwards and three generation downwards of the generation divided into each of the male and female domains. Among the male progenitors from the father's side we have- *Pita/Bap/Babu* (*Pita*), *Dada* (*Pita-ka-Pita*), *Pad-Dada* (*Pra-Pita-Pita*). These have their respective feminine forms in *Maa*, *Dadi* and *Pad-Dadi*. The descendants in the chain include - *Poot/Beta* (*Putra/Batuka* or *Vatsa*). *Pota* (derived from *Putra* through *Vridhi*) and *Pad-Pota* (*Pra-Potra*). The female versions (*Beti/Dhih*, *Poti* etc.) have been derived by adding feminine suffixes except in the case of *Mata/Maa* which is a primary kin name for obvious reasons. It is interesting to note that though there is a fourth kin nomenclature on either end of the chain viz. *Sad-Dada/Dadi* and *sad-Pauta/Pauti*, such kins are hardly countenanced and in some quarters these kins are taken as unwelcome. The reason for such a belief could be the chances of such a patriarch rotting after certain age in most cases, our Vedic prayer of '*Jivema Sharadah Shatan*' notwithstanding.

Among the kin names of progenitors from mother upwards are -*Nana* (*Nanri*), *Pad Nana* (*Par Nanri*) yielding the female versions *Nani* and *Pad-Nani* by adding feminine suffixes. Looked at from the upward scale, the kin names do not go beyond one generation of *Dauhata/dauhati* (*Dauhitra/Dauhitri*) as hardly any interaction takes place between the succeeding kins. Here we may cite the riddle popular among rural folk viz. "*do ma-beti aur do ma-beti chali bagh mein jaan, teen nimboo tod ke saabat saabat khan, batao kaise?*" Evidently they are–the mother, her daughter and daughter's daughter, three in all.

Then there are horizontal blood kins both from the side of father and mother. Elder brother of father gets the term *tau* (*Pitrivya*) and that younger to him is known as *Kaka/chacha* (*Kanishthaka*). Father's sister is *Bua/Phuphi* (*Pitri-svasa*) Mother's sister, elder or younger has same term *Mausi* (*Matrisvasri*). *Mama* (*Matula*) is the nomenclature for Mother's brother. Males born of the same parents are to each other *Bhai* (*Bhratri*)

Bira (*Vira*) if Male and *Bahan/Bahen/Jiji, Bebe* (*Bhagini*) if female. Children born of a brother of get the term *Bhatija* (*Bhratrija*) if male and *Bhatiji* (*Bhratrija*) if female. Sister's husband is known by the term *Behnoi/Jija* and her children get the nomenclature *Bhanja* (*Bhaginija*)/*Bhanji*.

In the category of affinal kins we have relationships established through marriage. First we talk of kins through marriage of self. The first kin in this way is the spouse - *Pati* (*Pati*) if male and *Patni* (*Patni*) if female. There are several *Desi* versions of such terms e.g. *Ghar ala/wala*, *Khasam*, *Mard*, *Log/Vara* if male and *Ghar wali/ali*, *Zoru*, *Bir*, *Lugai*, *Bahu/Bahuria* (*Vadhu*) if female. Husband's father is *Susra* (*Shvasura*) and his mother is *Sasu* (*Shvasru*) and similar are the terms vice-versa. The parents of the spouses have their relationship to each other described by a common nomenclature of *Samdhi* (*Sambandhi*) if male or *Samdhan* (*Sambandhini*) if female. A son-in-law is *Jamai* (*Jamatri*) and daughter-in-law is *Bahu* (*Vadhu*). Interestingly brother's or sister's mother-in-law is called *Mausi* (*Matrisvasri*) bringing her at par with one's own mother and the masculine derivative *Mausa* is for father-in-law. In reciprocity the son-in-law's brother and sister are given the nomenclature *Sambdheta* (*Sambandi*)-*Batuka* and *Sambdheti* to be known via their father rather than through their brother. Husband and wife moving further in to each other's family circle receive separate kin names in each relationship. Thus we have husband's *Dada/Daddi* called *Dadasara/Dadas*, *Tau/Tai* as *Tayasara/Tayas*, *Kaka/Kaki* as *Pitasara* (*Pitrivyashvasura*)/*Pitas*, Husband's elder brother as *Jeth* (*Jyeshta*) and the latter's wife as *Jethani*. Similarly husband's younger brother and his wife are *Devara* and *Devarani* respectively. Husband's sister and her husband are given the terms *Nanand* (*Nanadri*) and *Nandoyya* respectively. Wife's brother is *Sala* (*Shyalaka*) and his wife is *slahaja* (*Shyaiakajaya*). Wife's sister is *Sali* (*Shyalika*) and her husband is given the appropriate term *Saddu* (*Saha-Wodha*) or *Humjulpha* in some circles. In olden times this kin was taken to be as good as non-kin and there was no independent interaction between the two except at family function like marriage at their common in-laws' place only. In modern times this affinal connections quite a hit. This is happening with the appropriation of due personal status to women accelerated by the emergence of the micro family and the impact of urban social norms on rural life and ways. Cousins and cross cousin are mutually addressed and treated mutually as brother (*Bhai*) or sister (*Bahen*) as the case may be. But for specific identification by strangers and third parties all relevant kin terms are employed in a composite form e.g. *Tau ka beta*, *Bua ka beta*, *Mama ki beti* etc.

Some kin terms have come to be used as pairs to denote closeness and mutual affection e.g. *Chacha-Bhatija*, *Bua-Bhatija*, *Mama-Bhanja*, *Babu-Beta*, *Ma-Beti*, *Devar-Bhabhi* etc. unfortunately *Sasu-Bhahu*, *Nanad-Bhavaj*, *Devrani-Jethani*, *Log-Lugai* are paired in not so flattering terms as can be gleaned from many a folk songs. But the helpless *Sasu*, mellowed enough through age and experience gets all the brick bats for the legendary atrocities committed on her daughter-in-law of which she herself had been a perceived victim when young. The system of cross cousin marriages in some communities, where a mother-in-law is either father's sister or mother's brother's wife, has perhaps behind it the factors of safety and security of the bride in this world of uncertainties. However, the Jats have ventured to merry away their daughters to far off places confident of the system of kinship that they have evolved by strict application of the norms of *gotra* exogamy and caste endogamy.

The above-mentioned kin names, though primarily evolved for specifically identifying the kins through relationship of blood or through connubial connection, are extended to a wider group of a village as a whole irrespective of caste and status. However, in case of reciprocity from the members of the *Brahmin* community there are certain exceptions. The norm is also in place in interaction with all known persons irrespective of the place they come from and irrespective of kin connections. In the latter case kin takes the form of geographic connection leading to social integration for civic life. This feature speaks volumes of level of equity observed by the Jats. Respective kin names of seniors are normally prefixed to names of person addressed from a distance and invariably used for addressing a person face to face- single or in company. Between cousins the term for addressing is brother (*Bhai*) or Sister (*bhen*/*Bebe*) as the case may be but the compound kin terms like *Tau ka Beta*/*Beti*, *Bua ka Beta*/*Beti*, *Mama ka Beta*/*Beti* etc. are employed to identify the relationship to third party. Strangers also get addressed with select approximate kin names determined roughly through analogy of age and appearance. Some of these are- *Dada*/*Dadi*, *Tau*/*Tai*, *Bhai*, *Beta*, *Beti*. It is to be noted that in this category we do not have *Bhabi* and *Bahan*/*Bahen*/*Bebe* as both these kin names are to be determined in relation to *Gotra*, which can be ascertained if we come to know a person closely.

Then we have several situations in life when kin names are used not for indicating kinship but to connote different meaning, these can be listed below:-

i) For adding emphasis in assertions or refusal- 'This time I wont leave this fellow (*Sala*) unpunished'; 'I shall give nothing to this fellow (*Sala*);

ii) For extending grudging admiration- The fellow (*Susra* or *Sala*) is indeed honest;

iii) For hurling abuses several kin names are freely used. Mother (*Maa*), Sister (*Bahen*), wife's brother (*Sala*), Daughter (*Beti*/*Chhori* suffer the worst when these terms get used in incestuous terms, especially at the hands of males. Among women *Bhabi* is a favourite term of abuse when used for quarrelling adversary. One is left wondering what two women in quarrel mean when they call each other '*Sasu ghadoun ki'* (Mother-in-law of horses). Cursing in the name of kins is a common feature but '*Bhai Roi*' '*Napooti*' (sonless) are the most hurting as they target the closest kins, a brother and a son.

iv) For adding emotion in folk songs of women sung on the occasions of marriage and festivals like *Teej* and *Raksha Bandhan* (Salonon). When a Bride embarks on taking the rounds of the sacred fire along with the bride groom the women folk present at the marriage ceremony synchronise singing the conventional song reminding her in each round of her kin connections (*Dada ki Poti*, *Babu ki Beti* etc.), thereby assuring her of their support at the most critical juncture of her life. The terms *Babu* and *Ma* have a nostalgic touch when rendered as *Babul* and *Mayad* respectively by a daughter in a far off place.

v) For entreatingly persuading someone who is not a kin, to do a favour – '*Tau aage ne ho le*'; '*O Phupha maan jaa*'. Such usages are taken sportingly by all concerned with a touch of amusement. Kin names are uttered even to adamant domestic animals to relent to do certain commands when patient cajoling fails to deliver. *Bhenoyen* (not *Bahen*!) are commonly used in such situations.

vi) Though basically appropriately used for a stepmother the term *Mausi* has borne stigma in context of supposed ill treatment meted out by her to stepson/daughter. Thus we have the phrase '*Sapon ki Mausi*'.

The order of precedence among kins is determined on the basis relative position on the hierarchical ladder. In case of a tie the one through blood connection takes precedence over the one through connubial connection. Parameters of precedence include- right of passage, order of greeting, position of seat on head-side or foot-side of a bed, obligation to hold a *hukkah* at the calf region (*gatta pakadna*) and offering it to others present, right to draw the inaugural pull at the same, representing the family/clan at *panchayat* etc.

A closer look at the kin names would show the following as the primary or basic terms:

Among the terms for blood relation there are four: (i) *Pita/Bap /Babu* (ii) *Mata/Ma/Maan* (iii) *Poot/Beta* (iv) *Beti/Dhih*. All other kin terms either upward in the scale or downwards both on the father's side and the mother's side are derived from these four.

However, one has to stretch one's imagination in deriving *Nana* from *Matri-Pita*. On the face it appears to be a vestige of the original Sanskrit term *Nanaanri*, gone obsolete with the passage of time.

In the same way we have the following basic terms among affinal kins: (i) *Pati/Vara/Log/Khasam* (ii) *Patni/Bahu/Lugai/Zoru* (iii) *Susra* (iv) *Sasu* (v) *Samdhi* (vi) *Samdhan*. Considering (iv) and (vi) as the feminine forms of (iii) and (v) the basic number comes to four. As in the case of blood relation the terms for other affinal relations are derived from these for.

Needless to say that the above system of kin nomenclatures has stood the test of time in keeping our social organization not only intact but also integrated, serving as a renewal system in the manner of rolling the past and unfolding the future for millenniums. With the growing urbanization and changing life patterns the system is already under strains. Our younger generations given to cosmopolitan way can hardly help being part of the anonymous system of individualism where distances are getting reduced with the introduction of faster means of transpiration but kins are getting more distant. We have very little time these days to refer back to the extended family and the entailing network of kins. But no one would deny admitting experiencing deepest joy on discovering and meeting a distant relation of several generations past.

15

Religion-Education-Nation

Humanity's best innovation, religion is the most important single factor in revolutionising human life. Practical application of religious teaching is needed to revolutionize our subconscious world. Such teachings are imbued with the power of the greater universal life behind all individualized, manifested life. A person who has undergone a human evolution on the deepest level of his consciousness knows how to relate with nature and fellow human beings. He knows that man must strive to remain in harmony with the forces and cycles of Nature. That alone would be the true path to tread in the pursuit of religious merit.

Second in importance to religion in bringing about the human revolution is education. Unfortunately, education today leans too far in the direction of imparting bare knowledge and neglects instruction in basic attitudes towards all human life, including knowledge. The amount of valuable learning, retained by young people today is disproportionately small in comparison with energy expended in acquiring it. Moreover, for the sake of imparting this knowledge, which may or may not be fruitful later on, we sacrifice truly important instruction in basic human values and attitudes.

Even the highest levels of education are less valuable than they might be if they are not complemented by learning geared to the complex and changing realities of our total environment. It will be a contradiction in terms to say that a person is highly educated but does not recognise a value structure in his thoughts and actions. And yet such contradiction is pervasive world over in the domain of education, which has been taken to be synonymous with instruction. Education with accumulation of degrees, professional or otherwise is perceived as a ladder to reach the heights of wealth and pelf with little concern for human values. The scenario in our country is all the more tragic. While on the one hand the highly educated here, generally finds himself at odds with the still lingering age old traditions which for centuries have held society together, the so called leaders of religious traditions are blindly pursuing the path of sectional aggrandizement resulting in social fragmentation on the other.

The modern educational system in India has evolved through western intervention mainly with the purpose of creating a workforce to serve the cause of British hegemony. The western model, which in turn had evolved out of its religious institutions, obviously had no reference to the concepts and precepts of the Indian religious tradition. The growth of scientific and technical education unaccompanied with moral teaching led to the superseding of whatever little was possible in the humanities stream. The policy planners in education sought to solve the problems arising out of the complexities of multi religious and multilingual society by keeping education distant from religious influences. The laurels earned by the surface success of this approach served as an impetus to the romantic liberalism of newly independent India. Oblivious of the superficiality of this success we chose to ignore the need of food for the soul. The side effect of this was the charting out of a fundamentally parochial course on the part of peripheral sections in almost all religious communities in our country. Initially seeking to fill the gap in the educational content by setting up institutions, these elements with the passage of time became perpetrators of inter-religion hatred and strife. The ironical part is that the most deprived sections of our society having little contact with modernity happened to be the clients victims?) of such institutions. The situation has not only continued to prevail in the realm of horizontal expansion of education but has been complicated multifold in a climate of politicking on the part of unscrupulous aspirants of power. Denominational schools and other institutes have mushroomed all over our country leading to diversity at the cost of unity.

Having achieved independence through mass struggle led by Gandhiji, adoption of a democratic system with universal adult suffrage was the only and the-natural way of governance for our country. Competitiveness in elections was hinged on issues of general concern in the earlier phases of the functioning of democracy. Ideology based on economic approach continued to be the corner stone of the declared policies and manifestos of contenders for political power. The hold of the leaders of the freedom struggle on the hearts of the masses was impregnable. The occasional ripples on the otherwise placid stream were ignored being taken as aberrations rather than seen as signals of undercurrents of serious nature.

Successive governments led by the same party and headed by the same leader for a considerably long period stupefied people. The stifling economic policies could not match up to the aspirations of the masses. Their raised expectations fanned by the euphoria and nostalgia of socialism and slogans of *Garibi Hatao* speedily turned into cynicism. Contending political leaders aspiring for power having failed to achieve their goal (of capturing power) through legitimate constitutional means became desperate and plunged headlong into a game of engaging the government in a 'direct' action in the manner of a war where no scruples or care for the constitutional methods was a bar. Boundaries of political ideology crashed and fora of high sounding 'principles' were floated to give cover to the self- aggrandizing actions of the leaders. Inflated egos of some celebrated leaders who had failed to engage themselves in nation building responsibilities even when invited by people in power at different times, found instant satiation from the showers of paeans of praise by the very political groups and formations, whom they had ever abhorred. Anarchic conditions were sought to be created to force the government's hands either to take drastic action against them or to quit. Either way the government would be the ultimate looser, they thought. Declaration of internal emergency in June 1975 was the consequence. Education had not succeeded in bringing maturity of our minds. We as a nation could be herded around by a sycophant bureaucracy awaiting a curious role.

Many of the leaders of the contending side were interned. In the process some innocent and peace loving citizens also found themselves in detention behind the bars. To make the people in general feel comfortable with the emergency regime several schemes of poverty alleviation and national reconstruction were put into place. The measure delivered on many fronts and people in general found their life a little more comfortable. Trains and buses ran on time. But soon we ran into a disaster when over enthusiastic organs of the state failed to perceive the sensitivity of a very personal and private affair and forced its pace in terms of statistics through coercive measures. The people of the villages and small towns in particular who were otherwise happy with the measures taken by the government during the emergency rose almost in revolt against this single measure of family planning clumsily implemented.

The damage had been done. There was no repair possible in quick time. Emergency was lifted and elections were called in the hope that impressed by the much touted welfare schemes the party in power would be voted back by the people. This assessment was proved wrong. The subterranean angst which had been lurking in the hearts of the common people gave expression through the ballot. The ruling party lost badly in the north which in particular had experienced the pinch of the 'family planning' programme. Though the party did rather well in the south it lost power in the centre in March 1977. What succeeded it was a combination of disparate groups with divergent ideologies and conflicting personalities. Internal squabbles and personable ego clashes among several members of the government led to its fall within a period of one and a half year of its assuming office.

The government that followed did not last long as it stood on borrowed legs. Not amenable to compromise on certain principles the government resigned and elections were called for early January 1980. The party heading the previous government returned to power with a comfortable margin riding on the wave created by the slogan of 'elect the government that works.'

But who would allow the government to work. India by that time had become almost ungovernable. Among other problems facing the country terrorism in Punjab assumed dangerous proportions. A religious leader had become a law into himself.

He challenged the government of the day to dare stop him from the course he had chalked out. He ensconced himself in the holy precincts of the Golden Temple and perpetrated acts which by no measure could be called holy. There was a strong demand for action against the religious leader who continued to be defiant and was reported to be toying with the idea of declaring the holy shrine area as an independent state with the promise of recognition and support from Pakistan. The circumstances compelled the government to act. There was military action at the shrine. Save the temple several structures surrounding it, including the seat of Sikh temporal authority, the Akal Takht, were reduced to rubble. It was 6th June 1984. The Sikh psyche was deeply hurt. All kinds of elements found an excuse for acting irrationally. Two Sikh guards posted to protect the Prime Minister Mrs. Indira Gandhi felled her with gun shots on 31st October 1984. On 1st and 2nd of November 1984 senseless killings of several thousand innocent and particularly poor Sikhs took place in several parts of Delhi and elsewhere. The saving grace was that many Hindus came forward to save many Sikh families from coming to harm. The crowds which were engaged in the killing were anonymous. But there remains little doubt about their class composition. It is ironical that they themselves were poor and it can't be any ones' case that they killed for wealth, since the victims had possessed very little. I believe it was lack of education, culture and finesse which was responsible for such a crude response to a sort of national tragedy. Such responses do not go to strengthen a nation. But we have learnt no lessons, either from the tragedy or from its aftermath.

We have continued to harp on divisive ideologies and in the process have found ourselves disagreeing on everything and every time. National harmony and unity in diversity have taken a back seat. We are not agreed on what directions our education system should take. The stereotypes about several sections of our own nation perpetrated by alien rulers and religious oppressors were continued to be passed on to our young minds in schools by the intellectual leaders who are supposed to know better. Ironically they failed miserably. Presumably they had not learnt their lessons of history really well. They being the leaders in education were supposed to dig deep and build anew the edifice of national education on a strong foundation rather than feign the debris as the doorstep of education. The frequent changes in government in the recent past, has further confounded the confusion. There have been elements at the helm of decision making in education who have wished to throw away the debris along with the inmates of the earlier edifices, no matter what loss the nation might suffer. They would also like to translate everything of the past into a language of their own which nobody else could understand. University curriculum would be decided upon by those who never went to a university but had religiously attended the open air gymnasiums with closed minds imbibing what was told to them as gospel. And the saddest part is that they mostly comprise good people, helpful to others. On the other hand those who stood against these elements did no better either. In the name of secularism they ought to place everything having any connection with Hinduism in the realm of their opponents leading to a gross distortion of what constituted nationalism.

Our path therefore, needs to be pruned of the weeds and thorns that have cropped up over the centuries in order to find our true bearings in search of the glorious humanistic traditions for the enrichment of our present. We must strive to discover, appreciate and propagate the essential unity of all religions; and work for a system of education which delivers us from all prejudices and enables us to be equipped with all relevant knowledge as valuable assets for the nation.

16

Snippets from Village Life of Yore

There were times when most of India lived in village. Self-sufficiency and interdependency among the different communities of a village was the hallmark of life of the people. Not clime but climate determined the ways of the people. Nature was their teacher from whom they had learnt to harmonize ever since the time of the Vedas. Modernity lived not in the life styles of the people but in their minds. With the advent of science and proliferation of related Technology rural life is changing fast, and no doubt for the better. But at the same time a grim picture emerges of the dilemmas confronting the ruralites in maintaining their customs and traditions to which they have been wedded for centuries. Their level of development has not reached nor appears to reach the stage when they can afford to fall in line with the ways of the cities. Communities like the Jats having strong *gotra* and kinship mooring based on ancient *Shastric* traditions find it still harder to deal with the unfolding scenario. But who knows, the future may throw up solutions which we may not imagine today. But we know that our yester years were somewhat different from what they are today.

For the benefit of our younger generation we give below a few snippets from the life in villages of the not so very distant past.

Harvest Time

Participation in the agricultural operation according to one's capacity was both a responsibility and an opportunity to learn the skills, which would stand in good stead in later life. Work here was a way of life rather than a burden. Leisure and entertainment was integral to daily life and socializing took place as a matter of routine without people making special efforts. Though there was broad division of roles, especially among the male and female members of a family, there were some operations, which needed the joint and concerted participation of all members-young and old. At several stages additional help was procured by hiring labourers from the non-agricultural lower castes not engaged in any independent economic activity. Harvesting was one such occasion. Wages to the labour force were given in kind on the basis of a percentage of the total output of the concerned worker. In addition food for mid-day meal served at the site formed part of the wages. Such arrangements took care of the escalation in prices of grain: To work out the percentage a unit method was used. For example, at a percentage of 8.33 every twelfth sheaf of the crop harvested would go to the labourer concerned. Continued vigil was required to ensure that no labourer indulged in the malpractice of making every twelfth bundle of the harvest unduly heavier and bulky in comparison to the other bundles. If any such malpractice was noticed the proprietor farmer had the right to replace the concerned bundle by any other. After harvesting the wheat crop the small bundles were heaped in a rectangular stack *(chhour/chhouri)* to be later transported to the threshing floors *(pair)* in the outskirts of the village. In case of the bundles of gram no such stacking was done at this stage. After waiting for some time for the bundles to dry the same were picked one by one and put into a moving cart and then taken to be stacked in a heap at the threshing floors. This method was resorted to in order to avert loss of grains in frequent handling of the fragile stalks, in subsequent operations it became easier to sift the grain from the chaff in case of the gram crop. Wheat crop however, entailed a more elaborate process to get the final yield. In case of both types of the crop the final stages saw the harnessing of several bullocks and buffaloes intertwined in an array to pound the stock under their hoofs. Men standing on a tripod would pour, down contents of bucketfuls sent up by the supporting members. The gently blowing wind would carry the chaff away leaving the grain to heap just in front of the tripod. Simultaneously a senior member of the family, usually a lady would promptly and neatly keep the grain mound free from chaff using a broom of fine stalks *(manjan<marjni)*. The accumulated mound of grain *(rass<raashi)* would be measured by using a standard large sturdy earthen pot *(maap)*.

The artisans like the black smith, carpenter, the barber, the potter, the bangle man as also the representatives of castes providing services like scavenging got their share on the spot before the farmer carted the grain to his house. This constituted part of the *jajmani* and barter system-'payments in kind, receipts in kind'. These days threshers and other machines have made the job quite easy and quick and cash transactions have replaced those in kind. But the old system re-emerges in the form of welfare measures like food for work programmes and the institutionalized system of supplying free ration to certain cadres of the armed forces as part of wages in contemporary times.

Agriculture and animal husbandry were the two sides of the same coin viz. the village economy. Similarly grain and chaff both had equal importance. While the former was basic need for the human population, the latter was necessary for the subsistence of the cattle. Another component of the agricultural produce was the waste, which served as instant fuel, fodder, manure or raw material for several other products. Timely and abundant rains were a normal feature almost every year. Water table remained within easy reach. Sinking of wells either for the purpose of irrigation or for drinking water was not a costly affair. Several ponds circuiting the habitation area were features found almost in every village. Vegetation around the village and wastelands for grazing cattle were in plenty. Summer or winter or be it rainy season, life in the village was free from tension though full of activities. All this has undergone a sea change due to the degradation of environment, resulting from hectic urbanization and industrialization. Development has its rewards but not without the accompanying liabilities.

Sugarcane Crushers *(Kohlu)*

Sugarcane is perhaps one of the oldest plant among cash crops. It finds mention in the Vedas as *Ikshu,* the plant oozing honey. With improved irrigation facilities and adequate rainfall the farmers in the plains of North India as elsewhere have always preferred to go for sugarcane crop, which yielded a rich harvest. Improved qualities of the plant in one tract have attracted the attention of growers in other parts. Before the onset of the machine age and later day technology the farmers in the village formed their own small cooperative ventures street-wise to process the crop for obtaining jaggery etc. By the end of the nineteenth century the new cast iron *kohlu* had replaced the outmoded wooden version, which was proving quite expensive as it needed frequent repairs and replacements. The new metal machine was patented by Thomson and Myine and was lent on hire. It had three heavy rollers with gears on top and varying in size with the main roller moving with a long wooden bar (*pait*) fitted into a hub at its top operated for crushing sugarcane. The *Kohlu* was rolled by harnessing a pair of bullocks at the extreme end of the wooden bar to move round the *Kohlu* anti clockwise. An attentive fellow called *Muthia* would put the sugarcanes into the mouth piece of the *Kohlu*. A tin canister with a capacity of fifteen-kilograms was placed in a small pit below the mouth of the outlet channel from where the collected juice flowed down. This measure formed one unit for the purpose of determining shares of each member of the co-operative venture. A family could opt for contributing a certain number of units one round of roster of the members. The product obtained was divided in accordance with the proportion of the units a member held. The member put themselves in a queue and maintain the order throughout. Gap if any happening due to unavoidable circumstances was required to be filled post facto. The members shared pro rata the expenditure (mostly in kind) incurred on the operations including the wages of the labourers engaged. All accounting work was orally done with striking precision and authenticity. Sometimes, to make the process more intensive, the system was modified so as to tackle in one go the crop of the members turn by turn (*Bari lagana*), Such practices were adhered to towards the final days of the season presenting fine examples of mutual co-operation. These small manual sugar mills were features on the outskirts of every village. The winter sun added charm to their hospitable milieu. The partners in a venture stacked their stocks of sugarcane in earmarked individual enclosures forming a semi-circle. Thatched walls were raised behind each enclosure securing the sugarcane stack from pilferage or damage by wayward animals. Some people made cosy beds in their enclosures by spreading layers of begasse *(khohi)* and the soft dry leaves *(paatti)* of sugarcane. They were focal points of socializing among the village people joining in long drawn out sessions of smoking *hukka.* Young school children could be seen often utilizing the cosy corner of such station for preparing jaggery. The collected cane juice was poured into a large iron pan (primary) fixed along with another (secondary) atop a two holed cavity deep enough to hold sufficient fuel for heating the juice. One side of the cavity was covered with a wall with a narrow hole left for intake of fuel. The other end of the cavity took the shape of a tunnel opening skywards for serving as an exhaust chimney for the smoke and excess energy. The hot earthen smoke tunnel *(dhoondala)* used to be a favourite rendezvous where young and old thronged to beat the shivering cold, particularly during nights. It was here that an elderly member of the co-operative *Kohlu* distributed fresh hot jaggery in lumps of small measures to all present every evening.

The pigs reared by the *chuharas (Balmiki's)* got their share of the press mud (*maili*) discarded in the process of clarifying the boiling sugarcane juice with the sprinkle of sap of stalks of the *bhindi* (lady finger) plant used as catalyst to obtain neat jaggery. On some occasions carrots fixed in hooked iron rods were dipped in the boiling pan to obtain delectable delicacies. These co-operative ventures have almost disappeared with the mushrooming of large sugar mills in the nearby towns on the one hand and the scantiness of the sugarcane crops in many village on the other. Their old world charm was not lost even to a contingent of British Troops on the way to Delhi whom I recall having halted on a sunny day at one of these venues in my village way back in 1944 to relish a treat of chewing sugarcane. The crop of sugarcane is slowly vanishing from many villages because of paucity of irrigation facilities and intensive hard work involved.

Fairs and frays

The biannual fair held at village Kundal like at several other villages on *Shivaratri* was slowly losing its lustre due to the increasing contacts of rural folk with the towns and cities. Till about the middle of the last century it lingered to have some of the old charm with multitudes of people from different places in their colourful new clothes thronging the venue. Older people would recall the youngsters receiving as their pocket money of two *annas*

(1/8th of a rupee), which was however, enough for buying little bits of wares like toys or for stimulating the taste buds of the tongue with a feast at the *chaat* stall. Some kind of voluntary (not forced by any code) apartheid could be noticed at the fair. The members of the *Harijan* community by convention attended the fair towards the concluding hours when wares started selling at throw away prices. By this time most of the upper caste members would have left for their homes or made it to the arena *(dangal)* to witness the wrestling bouts invariably organized on such occasions. People were hailed to the venue with the beating of drums. The umpire not only conducted the bouts in according with norms announced in advance but also enforced discipline among the crowd gathered around the arena in clusters supporting one or the other fighter through specially appointed volunteers. Match making of each fight among the participants was made by the referee by mutual agreement between two of the wrestlers in the fray. The fights were conducted on a specially prepared pit filled with soft earth. An unwritten protocol of wrestlers was scrupulously observed by all participants. A spirit of sportsmanship and fair play prevailed throughout the events. A peculiarity of the *dangal* was that it used to be an all male affair. Women folk were not supposed to be there even as spectators. It was not for the reasons of male chauvinism but a discreet step to save women from the spectacle of little clad muscular bodies of the contestants. Segregation of sexes, in any case, was a general norm in the life of village folk those days. Moreover, the concept of the brave knights winning the fairies did not touch Indian life. *Chivalry* was not a matter of public demonstration for the people. Here we subscribed to the idea of *Veerbhogya vasundhara* (the brave rule the earth). The fair held annually on the compound of the religious seat of the *Sadhs* in village Nahri used to be a bigger draw.

Food and Drinks

In olden days village life was as a whole integrated with the environment in all its aspects. Food was based on local agricultural products. The *rabi* crops yielded the major grains of wheat and gram as the mainstay of the food item round the year also providing some surplus for marketing to raise cash. The *karif* crop was short lived and yielded grains just sufficient enough for change of taste to the palate for a couple of months in winter. *Chapaties* made of millet flour to be had with vegetable prepared from the tender leafy stalks of mustard plants with lumps of fresh white butter on top used to be real treat. *Khichdi* made from pounded bits of millet laced with a rich serving of clarified butter was a favourite dish in almost every household of the village at dinner time during the season. In summer breakfast constituted of *chapaties* made of wheat flour mixed with a sprinkling of gram flour. Butter milk in abundance was available for topping up according to the needs and liking of an individual. Onion was there at any meal time as it was generally home grown. Lunch time menu included *Chapaties* made of wheat flour with some vegetable or *dahi,* generally of local product. In summer *rabari* (wheat flour soaked in yogurt cooked after fermentation) was a hot favourite, especially the overnight saved scruff mixed with yogurt to be savoured the next morning. In case of the vegetable items there used to be great amount of give and take between close neighbours. The universal potato was easily available and stood in good stead in cases of emergency. During their spare time on sunny days in the rainy season women folk used to prepare *seviaan* from clods of thick paste of fine wheat flour placed on top of earthen pots turned upside down. Dinner time was *dalia* (porridge) time. It was cooked from pounded bits of wheat painstakingly obtained through a long process-soaking the grains in water for some time, placing the same on a cloth spread on a cot till it dried half, pounding gently to let the crust shed off, then winnowing it to obtain fine grain, and finally vigorously pounding with a heavy wooden staff *(musal)* the grains placed in a deep cylindrical stone container *(ukhal)* to get a ready to cook stuff. The preparation was on different day by rotation sweet-mixed with jaggery, salty or just plain to be left to the choice of the individual member of the family to have it sweet or salty. Festival time saw ladies preparing dainty dishes of *halwa puri and kheer* and the added specialities were *gulgule* and *poodey* if it happened to be rainy season. *Suhalies* were deep fried small cakes prepared from a hard thick paste if wheat flour mixed with jaggery solution. This preparation lasted months and therefore was prepared in large quantities. Bag full was dispatched to the home of married daughter. Youngsters would tuck a piece or two in their pockets when going out for playing out to savour the same in case they felt hungry. *Laapsi* was the fat free version of *halwa* with jaggery replacing sugar as sweetener. It could be called a poor man's *halwa.* Today village is no more cut off from the ways of life in the cities and towns. Only the sophistication is lacking, the polish is not there. Means of communication and transport have bridged the gap substantially. Proximity with Delhi has opened avenues of employment in government and private sectors to many a people in the villages. Most of them being daily commuters to and from the city serve as carriers of the latest trends in food habits from the city to the village. At marriage parties also the menu is usually a carbon copy of what one finds in the city though *laddoo* and *zalebi* continue to rule the roost. Of course *guldạna* has almost disappeared from the table and similar is the fate of vegetable made of *kaddu* along with the delectable *chatni* of *kalonji* so painstakingly prepared by the local *halwai.* The aroma of smell of leaf plates and cups is missing as these have given place to the exotic items of crockery linked with status. Similarly the buffet system has taken away the sweet side of hospitality oozed at the guests by bands of young men serving entreatingly the different items of the menu at the feasts. The event today has turned impersonal and the guests hardly have a chance to relate to the hosts. The aura of getting served entreatingly is missing in marriage feasts these days. Water was the main drink. It was served sweet mixed with country made sugar. In summer some enterprising hosts arranged for ice from the nearby towns. The modern beverages had not reached the village. Consumption of liquor was rare and was discreetly kept a private and personal affair in a manner that those who did not indulge in it, hardly got a smell of it. Today we find a sea change in the matter of food and drinks among the village folk. We find hardly any difference between the city life and that in the villages. Attend any marriage party in a village and find every item of food that you were accustomed to part take in a party in the city. We can say to our young generation that the change is for the better. But we would also say that they should also know what we were yesterday so that we may visualize our tomorrow.

17

Custom, Law and Gender Conflicts: Resolving the Jat Way

The concept of moral law was known to the Indo Aryans at a fairly early period. The vedic people called it *rita* and the *Avestans* knew it as *Asa.* According to the Rigveda the universe was an ordered whole. The ways of life of good men who follow the path of *rita* was called *vrata* (Rigveda IX.121.1; X.37.5). The concept of cosmic law continued to dominate Indian thought but the term *rita* was rarely used to express it leaving the idea to be expressed by terms like *karma* or *dharma.*

The word *dharma* has been found used in the sense of law. Veda is said to be the source of all *dharma (vedo dharmamulam (Gautama Dharmasutra-1.*1.2) and *Vedo=akhilo dharmamulam smritishile cha tadvidam. (Manu-*2.6) The Rigveda uses the terms *prathamo dhramah* (3.17.1; 10.56.3) and *Sanatana-dharmani* (3.3.1). in the sense of the first laws and the ancient laws respectively. The word *dharma* is used variously but the central meaning of a definite injunction or rule or some kind of arrangement remains the common strain throughout.

In the context of property rights we have this from the *Taitiriya Samhita* (3.10.9.4): *Manuputrebhyo dayam vyabhajat* (Manu apportioned property among the sons). The same text (2.5.2.7) talks of the inheritance of the eldest son. Rigveda (8.30.3) contains a prayer for not digressing the path of the ancestors laid down by Manu (*ma nah pathah pitryan manavadadhi duram naista paravatah).* The Taittiriya Samhita (2.2.10.2) says whatever Manu said is medicine *(yadvai kincha Manuravadat tad bhaishajam).* Similar is the declaration of Tandya Brahmana (*Manurvai yatkinchavadat tad bheshjam bheshajatayai).* So we note that matters like ownership of land, inheritance and partition of property did concern the ancient vedic society as much as they do today.

The concept of four ends of human life *(purusharthas)* viz. *dharma* (piety), *artha* (wealth), *kama* (fulfilling desires) and *moksha* (liberation) to be pursued in order of precedence as listed, serve as fair guide to regulate human life in an orderly fashion. Laws framed in deference to this precedence serve[1] the need of society in a better way.

Thus we can say that judicial administration among ancient societies was nowhere as well established as in India. The king was the source of law and he in turn depended on a well laid down procedure and rules concerning the various spheres of human behaviour. It was neither possible nor desirable to have a consolidated code in one compendium. The varieties in local traditions and despotic nature of the state did not countenance a monolithic judicial code. However, the extent *Dharmaṣāstric* literature along with the *Arthaṣāstric* tradition has evidence enough to show that the Indians had so thoroughly applied their mind on the basis and nature of law relating to both civil and criminal spheres of human behaviour from a fairly ancient period. The Manu Smriti has prime position followed by *Yajnavalkya, Narada* and *Bṛhaspati Smṛti* dealing with different topics of ancient Indian law.

The Manu Smriti gives four sources of law viz. 1. *Shruti* or the *Vedas,* 2. *Smriti,* 3. *Custom* and 4. One's own inclination. Manu clarifies that in case of conflict *Shruti* will prevail over *Smriti* and both these will have precedence over the last two. According to *Yajnavalkya* the law of the *Smritis* is the law enforced by the courts of justice. The same is supplanted by equity and custom. No wonder then that enlightened rulers even among the aliens in appreciation of the well-established judicial tradition in India tried to formulate laws as far as possible in sync with the prevailing customs and practices. Thus we find the great Mughals issuing *farmans* and *sanads* granting some level of autonomy and privileges to the *khap panchayats* in matters governing the socio-religious life of the people. Similarly the British found it expedient, to largely draw upon the ancient Indian law books like the Manu Smriti to frame the code for governance of India. India being a vast country of heterogeneous character in matters of laws on inheritance and succession as per local custom the British had not tinkered with the customary law. Modernity of the west was not sought to be implanted for obvious reasons. What did not concern them did not pinch them was perhaps the case even in the face of stark distortions that had taken place in certain laws based on custom. More poignant was the situation arising out of the denial of the right of inheritance to the female progeny in landed property in various parts of the country. The customary safeguards evolved by the older generations had sadly been long abandoned.

It was therefore natural that independent India took early steps in reforming several laws to mitigate the situation. Though the initial attempt in the amorphous form of the famous Hindu Code Bill met with stiff opposition from no less a person than the then President of India Dr. Rajendra Prasad. What followed was the piecemeal enactment of the spirit of the original bill. The amended land laws brought up by the Punjab government presented a unique dilemma before the peasantry in north India, especially the Jats who have been the principal inheritors of the traditional vedic ways of life. The grant of the right of inheritance in land to the girl child on the one hand was seen to provide the much needed succour to the family with no male child it gave occasion to sow seeds of distrust and dissension among sister and brother. Since the system in the latter case sought to take away what was sought to be given away-the bride givers being compensated when they take the role of bride takers. In the former case what was apparently seen as a measure for female empowerment turned out to be almost a fiasco. Land being an immovable asset the inheritor female could not control or properly manage it unless she left her marital home and settled on her parental land, an option leading to several complications of social behaviour so vital in a rural setting. Such female inheritors of their parental land tended to sell it off and quit leaving behind bitter co-laterals snapping all kinship ties only to be missed on all social occasions. We are quite familiar with emotional strands that are witnessed on occasions like *Bhat* when sisters eagerly await their brothers' arrival.

How custom has scored over law is well demonstrated in the way the Jats have responded to the situation wherever the inheritance law has been amended to grant right of succession to the girl child. The general trend noted among the Jats of Haryana is of sisters voluntarily coming forward to give up their rights in favour of their brothers at the time of the partitioning of parental land. The dictum of quid pro quo has been well demonstrated in their approach. The scenario brings into sharp focus the fallacy of the rule of thumb enacted in the form of law in view of the situation on the ground. One way could be providing in the inheritance laws safeguards and security to a girl who has no brother surviving her. But at the same time ultimate alienation of land should be prevented.

Closely related to the above is the issue of the endemically disproportionate sex ratio in the demographic spectrum of the region where the Jats mostly abound. The phenomenon is attributed by observers, without citing any empirical data, to the practices embedded against the girl child-like female infanticide, wilful neglect of health care and nutrition in case of the female population in general and the girl child in particular leading to high mortality rate, elimination of female foetuses through abortions with the aid of modern technologies for sex determination and last but not the least the recourse to intervention of Indian system of medicine believed to be successful in ensuring male progeny in majority of cases. But it would be unfair to expect one to one ratio in respect of the two different sexes. Biological reasons could be responsible for the tilt in favour of the male child. After all countries like China and South Korea also do not show a better female to male ratio. Nearer home states like Maharashtra and Gujarat don't do better either. In fact there appears to be a north south divide in terms of sex ratio paradigm. The unequal ratio today is again not a new phenomenon in the north. The figures of the last century and more present almost the same unequal ratio showing bias against the girl child. Our past also hearkens us no less in craving for begetting the male child. The Vedic prayers abound in beseeching the gods for various favours, the one most frequently repeated being the one for having sons who would be brave and virile, capable to devour-the adversaries. The psyche of communities owning and living by land tilling is similarly fashioned to prefer a male child. The presumption of sex specific abortions needs to be established after a steady study of the analysis of under 10 population over a period of time. Such study would also be helpful in evaluating the efficacy of the law enacted by the state declaring prenatal sex determination test as criminal act.

A side light on the deteriorating female population in the northern and north western regions affecting the time honoured customs of caste endogamy and of limited geographical spread of marriages would be quite relevant here. There are frequent reports of young people across Haryana, unable to find brides nearer home or in their region, look for matrimony in far off regions in the south giving a neat go by to the time honoured customs. The implications of such marriages would come to the surface perhaps in their next generations. For the present such mongrel couples are reported to be doing well. Such marriages may prove an alternative to the difficulties in maintaining the rule of prohibitions of four *gotras* among the Jats who in several places are moving slowly towards consanguineous marriages by first (in the early last century) deleting the *gotra* of mother's mother's father and then later (towards the end of the last century) of father's mother's father from the prohibited list.

So we notice that in one instance law standing in way of custom is over ruled (hoodwinked!) by mutual consent and in another custom coming in the way of necessity supported by law is over ruled (bypassed!) again by mutual consent. But in both the examples we can read an under-current of inter dependency of the individual and the society. The Jats have proved themselves as apt in finding solutions to knotty problems as they have ever been doing in their vocation of farming and cattle rearing since ages.

18

Kinship, Custom and Hierarchy Among the Jats

Peasant communities like the Jats and other allied castes settled in the north and north-west India have continued to lead a fulfilling social life for millenniums. Their kin relationships cemented through a hierarchical arrangement evolved through natural inclinations and based on sound psycho-scientific principles have contributed to the emergence of numerous customs and traditions.

The parameters of kinship are multiple and all of these intertwined and come into play in a variety of ways depending upon their nature and the locale of their relative functionality. Kinship is fostered on the basis of the bonding by blood relationship and affinal/connubial relationship, the latter turning into the former category as soon as a married woman becomes a mother. It is made more broad based in certain areas of social interaction. The extended form of kinship applicable in the case of the residents of the same village to begin with is known as brotherhood *(bhaichara)* with the operation of several factors, the major being the commonality of *gotra*. The other factors are the geographical proximity leading to frequent interaction between the members of different villages working in adjacent farm lands. This is called *seem jod* brotherhood. Closely related to this is the brotherhood of *gohand*-the extent upto which the cattle of each other each for grazing. Then we have the brotherhood of *nyota nithar* built by some persons of one village with selected members of other village/s of the neighbouring areas in extending reciprocal invitations at feasts, especially on occasions like marriage irrespective of having different *gotra*. The code operating between two brothers is observed by all members of such brotherhood. Marriages are not contracted irrespective of the exemption available from the mandatory prohibitions of gotra. But it must be stated here that such brotherhood in most cases is found to be selectively and voluntarily forged except in case of matrimonial alliances where it takes a universal character.

Kinship through blood relationship may be a matter of accident of birth but kinship through connubial relationship being the vital cord of the social fabric is just not a result of matrimonial contrivance to be taken for granted to yield certain privileges. It is rather a tender plant to be nurtured assiduously and continuously throughout one's life through inputs both material and psychological by everyone when in the role of bride giver (which is the lot of almost everyone some day). Therefore, rural communities have evolved, through centuries, customs and practices, which have not only contributed to the enrichment of kinship relationships but have also gone a long way in making life purposeful and enjoyable.

Thus we have the kins on the bride givers' side willingly and happily coming forward with best possible gifts for the new born baby of their daughter/sister along with presents for all kins in the new family. As the major items of clothes are supposed to be of yellow colour the custom is called *Pilia dena.* Married sister living in the same village or a nearby village also visit the newborn male child and offer gifts in cash and clothes and some ornament. This custom called *Rupayya Potada dena* has in the modern times, turned into a real pompous affair. After the mandatory period of forty days of confinement the young mother visits her parental home and returns with a good amount of presents, mostly clothes and expensive ornaments for herself and in some cases also for her husband and sister-in-law/mother-in-law if the child was a boy. Since the custom is related to the time of *sutakant* (end of the period of confinement) is known in common language as *Chhuchhak*. By this time *Dusar* and *Teesar* have been dealt with by the parental side of a young wife incurring, ungrudgingly, a good amount of expenditure on clothes and other useful items. Come *Savan* (the month of plenty of rain) and the father-in-law of the newly married girl, still living with her parents heads for the home of his counterpart with bagfuls of sweet meats and new garments for his daughter-in-law as a good will gesture towards strengthening the kinship bond. This seasonal event would, in subsequent years, turn into a reverse visit of the bride's brother carrying similar gifts on the eve of the *teej* festival for the sister in her marital home. Since the gifts invariably included among other gifts a bagful of cookies like *suhalies* the visit got the name *Kothali lejana*. Of course, the bride giver brothers continue visiting married sisters carrying for them gifts (*Siddhha*) on the eve of all other festivals round the year. This system is geared towards nurturing and strengthening the kinship ties. However, it fades off slowly with the passage of time when the new generation takes over.

Bhat bharna is a major event when a brother accompanied by several kins comes to attend the marriage of a child of his sister. He offers a fair amount of cash according to his capacity and clothes for the bride/ bridegroom and members of the family. He also does not forget to offer a *rupayya* each to all the housewives of his village/*gotra* married in the village. In fact the custom is open ended for all occasions in case of cross cousins. The emotive value of the custom is far more superior to the financial support that it ensures. This is why we have the kins of the grandmother of the bride/groom chipping in for offering *Badabhat*, though discreetly modest not to excel the effort of the kins of the mother. In farming communities as elsewhere parents spare no efforts in getting for their daughter best possible grooms forgetting the financial burden they might have to bear.

Probably no one would disagree-that all these and many more customs cementing kinship bonding are a product of the natural process of social networking among the older communities otherwise leading a sedentary life. But it is generally less realized that they also reflect the psyche of equity among the bride givers who would like to compensate their daughter/sisters for their having surrendered rights in land notwithstanding the latest laws enhancing empowerment of women. A survey done of this phenomena could yield quite a revealing result. People of the non-farming communities, especially the elite among them would hardly be able to appreciate the nuances of this aspect of the ways of the Jats. It is true that land can be partitioned, but it is also true that land cannot be parcelled and dispatched to other quarters, even if it were to be the marital home of a married daughter/sister. Alternatively if the female were to come back and settle on the land of her share after partition of the parental land the very purpose of sending her away to another home is defeated bringing in its train the oddities of social etiquette in face of time honoured customs. A few examples of aberrations in the customs have-ended in disastrous results. The spectrum in urban areas is quite different, but the social fabric of rural India as of now for its very survival does not countenance thoughtless tinkering on the part of the State which does not think twice before throwing the baby away along with the bath water. Hasn't the experience of the so called modern societies shown that any imbalance between individual and social choices would lead to unhealthy consequences not good for either. A recent report of there being nearly 50% children born to unwed mothers in U.K. has set the Government and social scientists thinking seriously to meet the invasion of so called modernity. Custom if respected at least for its length of experience can serve better than a clueless law. The practice among village communities of arranging the marriages of their daughter at a fairly young age was, one can argue, an answer to several questions arising in the world of modernity today. The stereotype of taking early marriage as a sign of backwardness needs to be reviewed in the context of socio-biological sync.

Hierarchy is the key and basic factor common to both kinship and custom for their functionality and operation. Degree of kin relationships fashions the levels of hierarchy and for practicing it customs are developed. The dimensions of hierarchy are, indeed, innumerable which permeate the Jat life at several levels. To begin with the community finds itself deciding ungrudgingly to accept a place lower to that of the Brahmins in the hierarchy of the caste system. None would miss to notice the willing regard they show to the members of that caste by using the term *dada* while addressing them regardless of their economic status or comparatively junior age. At the same time the Jat does not forget to assert his hierarchy vis-a-vis the other castes. Above all the Jats consider the hierarchy of the *Panchayat* as sacrosanct and would go to any length to uphold its ruling. The Jats have, in the recent years, demonstrated a strong penchant for caste codes.

In the context of family the male with highest kinship degree takes precedence. The eldest son *(gotrapatya)* followed by younger son/sons if any and grandsons continue to wait in the wings as *Yuvapatyas* till their turn comes to fill the bill. Bride takers take precedence over bride givers among the kin relations. We often hear and ourselves repeat words like-*ham ladki wale sada jhukte hain:* Bride givers' grown up children part taking the left-over food (especially the *ghee* soaked sugar) of the visiting bride takers is perhaps indicative of the acceptance of higher hierarchy of the latter. There were times when the parents hardly visited their daughter in her marital home, and if some special circumstances took them there eating food at her quarter was a taboo, which however, was not the practice in case of kins of equal or lower degree like brothers and nephews. But there were occasions when the bride givers too called the shots. In older times when boys and girls, especially the latter were married off at a younger age the custom of *Theek* was in place. Before the young maiden was to be brought to her marital home for regular stay the husband had to visit (in some cases more than once) simply to fix the date (*theek karna*) when he could take her along. It used to be a tough mission for a young man to crack the stubborn posture of the canny mother-in-law for agreeing on a date. The spectacle of the young lass, more than keen to accompany her husband, eves dropping from behind some cover, holding her breath has given coinage to the following words depicting her dilemma: *Maa, ghaltee ho te mindhi chotti karoon, nahi te gitwad mein jake thepadi pathoon*-mother, tell me, if you are ready to send me with my husband, I get my hairdo; otherwise I go and make dung cakes in the yard. The parameters of hierarchy in kinship relations both in its narrow and wider sense can be described as follows:

Hierarchy of age is very important, it prevails in all situations accept where other well defined over riding factors come in to reckoning. Among equals in kinship degree age determines, as to who would take precedence on occasions like i) receiving greetings from younger people; ii) occupying seat on the head side of bed; iii) drawing the first (inaugural) pull at the *hukkah* in a gathering, the youngest of the lot is to operate the rotation; iv) representing the kins at marriages and other ceremonies; v) eldest male among the members of the *barat* receiving on the front at the shirt the customary stamp of palm dipped in *hina* given by the bride's mother at he send-off gathering; vi) among the ladies the eldest having the privilege of opening the knot of the loads of wares *(gathari kholana)* that a newly married woman brings to her in-laws family vii) and to set rolling the process of distributing the sweet meats contained therein. Interestingly the right to take precedence on the basis of seniority in age is mostly asserted with the declaration, '*tere se pahle anaj khana seekha tha*-I happened to taste grain before you could do it.'

Hierarchy of degree in kinship, though generally coinciding would over-rule the precedence given to age. An uncle may be junior in age to a nephew in extraordinary circumstances, but he would find a senior position in hierarchy. Progeny fathered in old age normally falls in this category. This way we find that heirship and hierarchy are inter linked closely. And last but not the least hierarchy comes into full play in the custom of observing of the custom of drawing the veil on the part of the Jat women when they appear before certain affinal kins.

It is a pity that not enough attention has been paid to the study of the sociology of the Jats on scientific lines. As bearers of a rich tradition of the vedic culture the Jats offer a gold mine of material for research. At least the universities located in the areas where Jats abound need to pick up the spade and start digging earnestly, and indeed deeply. Some German scholars have, during the past few decades, shown the way.

19

Let us Sow Seeds of Secularism to Weed Out the Creed of Terrorism

Terrorism has become the greatest scourge of civil society today the world over. But in India it has assumed very complex and awesome dimensions. Awesome dimensions, not because of the magnitude and frequency of terrorist driven acts and incidents, but because of the absence of a national consensus on the diagnosis of the reasons for the prevailing phenomenon and because of the almost bipolar nature of the remedies offered to cure the malaise. Whereas there are groups, in many cases organized as cultural fora and also as political entities, who sincerely believe it to be the product of civilisational (a cover for religious?) conflict, there are others, who taking a kind view of the eras of religious excesses as things of the past to be buried, plead for creating a new India where different religious and cultural identities could thrive together. But unfortunately both the above approaches are found least as societal concerns and most as state concerns. These include state concerns, both on the part of the groups in power and the groups aspiring for power. Societal ideology has almost become subservient to state concerns, which dominate most initiatives in any walk of life. The unending electoral syndrome has come to occupy disproportionate space in our national life and as a result we find hardly any time or occasion to sit back and talk of societal concerns transcending our smaller identities.

India has had a rich tradition of disputation and argumentation on individual level covering a wide range of human life and activities. In India of the glorious past the adversary real or feigned was almost a must for any serious discussion of an issue.

Even where there was none the disputant had to invent one as the *purvapaksha* (the opposite view).

But alas! Those engaged in the state sphere today are not only oblivious of the possibility of the other view being the right view but also are aghast when confronted with the other view as they claim to exclusively possess the gospel. All issues of social justice and economic equity are seen through the divisive prism emitting colours of 'pseudo secularism', 'appeasement' or 'communalism'. Things get worse when legitimacy of the fake is sought by manipulation of the electoral apparatus. In such an environment half-truths, rumours, muscle power and money power rule the roost, leaving the hapless moralists of all hues falling by the wayside. In some cases the contending parties when out of power, in desperation do not hesitate to indulge in what could be easily construed as anti-national and subversive activities in pursuing a perceived view of patriotism.

In the context of India, the most disheartening aspect is the utter lack of communication between communities. Leaving apart the tradition of Sikhs which many Hindus, especially Punjabis, fondly follow there is appalling ignorance about each other's religious beliefs and practices among the Hindus and the Muslims, excepting of course, the votaries of the composite culture, a contribution of the period of the great Mughals like Akbar and the Sufi tradition in Islamic annals. The hiatus prevails today in a more pronounced form reinforced by the contemporary trend of fragmentation of identities on grounds of religion, caste, language, region and even clans. The exclusiveness becomes more poignant when most of (or all of) the terrorists apprehended or killed turn out to be members of one particular community leading to a feeling of guilt or injured innocence. Those outside the community hasten to conclude the community as a whole as one responsible for the unfortunate incidents of terrorism. There are very few who can maintain a balance of approach towards the guilty and the innocent. Such an attitude can be cultivated only when we are intent upon arriving at the truth avoiding hasty conclusions driven by biases.

In this connection we can profitably recall what Ashoka the great had to say for bringing about communal harmony. Representing the state, he himself did not hesitate to reveal his own religious preferences, but at the same time he did not fail to appreciate the scenario of his empire being host to several religious and cultural communities. A fair deal to all was the *summun bonum* of his approach. "Let all sects live their own way (*sarve pashandah vaseyuh*)" was his basic premise to start with. He was aware that such a climate can be created only when we develop tolerance and respect for the tenets of others. So he went on to suggest the key for the same. It was restrain of speech (*vacho guptih)* when it came to talking about affairs of the sects of others. According to Ashoka at the root of all religious strife was the unbridled criticism of other religion or an exaggerated elation of one's own religion out of context, which he advised should be avoided (*atma-pashanda-puja va para-pashanda-garha va na bhavet aprakarane).* A great pragmatist as he was, Ashoka did not fail to recognize the hard reality of this being not always possible. So he hastens to add that if the context in a particular case demands (in an academic discussion, for example) that criticism of others' religion is necessary, one could proceed with circumspection avoiding extreme postures (*laghuka va syat tasmin tasmin prakarane).* At the same time he emphasises that one should not forget to show respect for others' religion wherever it was due *(poojayitavyah eva para-pashandah).* Acting otherwise was a sure way to harming one's own religion. Ashoka has a word of advice on how to develop tolerance in religious matters. According to him the secret lies in learning more about the tenets of other religions. Possibly, a well-informed person was less likely to indulge in irresponsible behaviour in religious matters. Millenniums have gone by since Ashoka's time but his words are relevant to our conditions today more than ever before.

If terrorism was the product of civilisational conflict, as some would believe, we would not have seen its heinous face in Muslim countries like, Pakistan. Morocco, Malayasia. Indonesia, Turkey and Saudi Aradia, and that too perpetrated by outfits constituted of local breed. In case of India our Prime Minister, with some sense of self elation had in a meeting with the American President last year observed that among the terrorist groups operating all over the world including those in India there was none who was an Indian national. Ironically, it did not take long to render this pious observation untrue. We have now a gallery of names among the terrorist organizations enlisting home grown terrorists masquerading with Indian labels. The recent revelations by Delhi police attribute the links of a large number of the young terrorists to a small place in Azamgarh in Uttar Pradesh. Similar is the latest discovery of the Bombay police. And the most disturbing aspect of the new groups is the young age and good educational background of their members professing Osama Bin Laden as their role model. To call them misguided innocent youth would be a self-defeating strategy to combat terrorism. But it would be a gross fallacy to paint the whole lot of Muslim youth with the same brush. If we consider the possible number among them engaging themselves in terror linked activities we may find its ratio to total Muslim population in India on a negligible low. Therefore, we must take utmost care in handling the phenomena. Whereas it is legitimate to apprehend, arrest and bring the terrorists to book through the process of law, we should make sure that we do not alienate our Muslim compatriots by generalizations and assumptions of guilt. If it were a religious activity we would not have seen many Muslims among the victims of the dastardly acts of terrorism. Alienation of a community does not contribute to the good health of a nation. The majority community has the onus to lessen the pain of minority syndrome in any given situation.

The example of America is before us to learn a lot from. The Muslims in America are not radicalised since they are well assimilated as Americans. In a recent poll as low a percentage as 13 justified the suicide bombings. The secular, middle class moderate profile of the American Muslim was certainly a factor not to be ignored in the reckoning of the pattern. We in India therefore, must work for creating conditions for the average Muslim to be counted not merely for his vote but for his own rights as a citizen of this common wealth, that is India. And for this we have to sow the seeds of secularism through our daily ordinary acts.

It is generally alleged that the alienation of the Muslim community is self-imposed as they huddle together in almost all walks of life. They prefer to live in exclusively Muslim enclaves, especially in cities, is cited as an argument. But we conveniently overlook the spectrum of Muslims in general not accepted as tenants in non-Muslim neighbourhoods. It is imperative that the syndrome of exclusivity, summed up by an Urdu poet in the lines *ham se bulaya na gaya, un se aya na gaya-needs* to be broken. What right some suspect groups have to appropriate to themselves the right to represent Hinduism or Hindustan? One may ask, Talks like-*Bharat mein agar rahna hoga, vande mataram kahna hoga*-are as injurious to the health of the nation as terrorism. It has to be remembered that there need be no contradiction between the Indian identity and the Muslim identity of the Indian Muslims as they could be (or should be) both at the same time. It should not be forgotten that Hinduism has the resilience to thrive in the midst of diverse identities. It is well known but scarcely highlighted that rural India serves as a bulwark against the monster of communalism. A few lessons could be learnt from such communities. The saddest part of our national life is that the media by and large highlights the negativities, which mostly represent the urban phenomenon and white collar attitudes.

The Muslims on their part have no less a responsibility, which I believe they are generally shouldering, to nurture the plant of communal amity. In this context the recent report (Times of India 7 October) of Bombay Police commissioner Hasan Gafoor should not go unnoticed. The report gives credit to ordinary citizens, especially those from the Muslim community, for providing key information that led to the arrest of 11 suspected 'Indian Mujahideen' terrorists from Pune, Mangalore and Mumbai. It will be more helpful if our Muslim brethren overlooked the religious identity of a terrorist and separated him from the community as they would any other criminal no matter what his motives are stated to be. No terrorist has a right to swear by his religious identity to harm his own country. No true Muslim would think of taking the life of innocents. Islam stands for peace.

Similar is the Christian question hogging anxious attention in some parts of our country. The self-appointed troopers parading the tribal areas for the avowed purpose of resurrecting Hinduism need to be reined in. Coercion in any form to reconvert the tribal people is as condemnable as the original act of forcible conversion. At this juncture it is for the tribal people as individuals or in groups to themselves decide how they would like to shape their religious life. These are not the times of creating monolithic religious communities. Hinduism has not only tolerated multiplicity of beliefs but has also created environment for the growth of variety in the manner of the Rigvedic dictum- *ekam sad viprah bahudha vadanti*-the same one truth has been represented by the learned in variety of ways.

The last but not the least to be emphasized is the need for building a consensus on nationalism transcending all communal concerns. The past should be seen in the light of such a consensus and not from the coloured eyes of political partisanism. Every nation has the right and privilege to glorify its heroes and their deeds of valour and sacrifices but if political labels of today are sought to be fixed on them with an eye on votes serious trouble is likely to arise. Discreet approach is a must in revisiting their activities lest the same should provide legitimacy to the creed of terrorism, albeit retrospectively. Gandhiji had fought the non-violent war for India's Independence not without a deep philosophical motive. Let us go back in history and hearken Buddha and Ashoka the Great. The secret of secularism lies at the tip of our tongue. Let us master it.

The ghastly killings by foreign terrorists-reportedly coming from Pakistan-in dastardly attacks in Bombay starting November 26 are not only unprecedented but also fall in a class apart. Mercifully the terrorists have since been eliminated. The Nation is in shock but ready to deal with the menace in the most appropriate and mature manner. Indian Muslim clerics have reportedly decided not to perform burial rites for the killed terrorists on Indian soil. This report should not go unnoticed. Further the fact that among the more than 180 innocent lives lost during the terror ordeal no less than forty were Muslims should suffice for us to say that the terrorists were not fighting for Indian Muslims. One can hope that our agony and anger over the tragic happenings, though legitimately expressed in outbursts against the ruling class, would in due course of time find channels, which would go to strengthen national solidarity and nurture secularism without fighting over the semantics of the term.

20

Shrinking Distances, Expanding Distancing

Paradigm Shift in Matrimonial Union Among the Jats

The Jats like other similar peasant communities in the North and North West India have, since ages demonstrated traits and characteristics in their social life reflecting a remarkable continuity of the *Vedic* and Sanskritic traditions. While on the one hand, they have been found adhering to the orthodoxy of the Vedic sacraments relating to marriage, on the other hand they are not found failing to sincerely having recourse to the code of the *Smritis* wherever the same answered their pragmatism. Forming matrimonial unions has engaged their best genius in institutionalizing it on sound scientific footings of ethnology, kinship hierarchy and geographical spread.

Generally settled as they were in clusters of *Gotras* in the rural settings, the rule of exogamy till not very recent times, led them to distant places to seek brides and to find matrimonial homes for their daughters, the difficulties and hardships of travel notwithstanding. They perhaps they believed along with *Rishi* Dayananda in the dictum laid down by Yaska in his Nirukta, a work on Vedic etymology, namely, *duhita doore hita* (a daughter better be married off to a distant place). We are hot unaware of tire distance angle through the traditional song of a daughter complaining to her father why she had been married off to a distant place, viz *babul! kahe ko byahi bidesh.* But we know that this long distance pattern was not devised as a negative feature. This must be understood in the context of the social milieu of the times, in a largely agricultural economy the chances of all the parameters of the respective parties (i.e. the bride givers and the bride takers) to be ascertained being limited, matchmaking was largely an impersonal matter to be personalized gradually with the passage of time. There being hardly any avenues like educational institutions for gainfully growing up as healthy adults, girls were married off at a fairly young age, though the formal married life was to begin much later at an appropriate age through the ceremony of *muklawa* (or *gona).*

The geographical spread of distance (at least in days when communication and transport were not easily available) served as a convenient buffer to ensure the privacy of the young couple awaiting, though not without settled assurance, to take responsibilities as husband and wife. This buffer of distance also served to guard the privacy of the two families. There were remote chances of news about any petty quarrel/islanders trickling down to each other's quarters through hearsay, thus narrowing the distancing in relationship and adding to the building up of family honour. According to a survey of the geographical spread of marriages in a particular Jat village during the early years of the last century had shown 15 to 20 miles (21 to 32 kilometres). Interestingly the average for ancillary castes like the carpenter, the barber, the blacksmith etc. had been shown to be higher. This can be attributed to the sparse distribution of population of these castes in different villages limiting their options of matchmaking by observing the general rules of prohibitions more or less similar to those observed by the Jats.

Times have changed. In spite of the accessibility and availability of faster means of transport and communication the community is seen to be preferring to have matrimonial unions at the shortest possible distance within the constraints of the traditional prohibitions. There too, we have noticed the progressive dropping or the four *Gotra* normas per convenience. The previous century saw the *Gotra* of the father of the mother's mother (i.e *Nani)* going out of reckoning among the prohibitions. The last century ended up with the widespread dropping of the *Gotra* of the father of the father's mother *(Dadi).* In case of neither of the instances there are known reports of relaxation by sanction of a caste *Panchayat.* Those settled in the urban areas do not have to observe the distance or neighbourhood norm. As long as the minimum *Gotra* exogamy norms are observed distance could be as close as next door. But there is a caveat. The norms of reasonable distance and *seemjod biradari* reckoned by the respective place of origin of the two sides would invariably be observed. Migration to the urban areas, even lock stock and barrel does not tear away the Jats from their caste moorings. It goes without saying that exceptions prove the rule and anonymous living is not the way for members of the community.

From the very early times the community had evolved an institutionalized system to ensure that there were no eases of either of the parties being taken for a ride, all along the distance that stood between them for quite sometimes, figuratively also. In older times the village priest (a *Brahman*) and the village barber-cum-go-between *(napita)* served as the marriage bureau. The two would combine and start exploring the possibility of match making on behalf of the parents of a girl in areas conforming to the requirements of the rule of *Gotra* exogamy and other apparent prohibitions like area of brotherhood either of common land boundary (*seemjod biradari)* or other proximity *(like nyota-nithar)* and land at some respectable distance at the place of their local counterparts. After working out a mismatch of the relevant information the members of the two bureaus would arrive at a possible settlement and call upon the family of the prospective bride groom and formalize the first step *(sagai*) of the union of the two families by offering rupee one as token in the presence of the representatives of the local community. With the passage of time the village priest got delinked from the process, for what reasons is difficult to say. Most probably it happened due to the impact of the Arya Samaj movement, which preached to practice Vedic prayer and *Yajna* even without the assistance of a *Brahman* priest. The last century itself, in its later years witnessed the village barber also taking a back seat. With the availability of faster means of transport and communication and wide, though slow spread of girls' education the parents came directly into picture. But the priest (not necessarily a *Brahman*) for sacrament and the barber as go-between have continued to stay at the centre of marriage ceremonies in all times.

With the shrinking of distances of marriages many aspects of the old world charm of bonding in kinship relationship is fast getting dull if not disappearing altogether. In older days large families qualified as preferred parties for forging matrimonial unions as marriage meant giving a daughter in a family. The bonding extended to members of the extended family on both sides. With the disintegration of the joint family, diversification of professions/vocations, spread of education among the female population and the impact of media have all contributed to the assertion of individualism among members of the community, especially the younger lot. With this we notice a trend of increasing distancing among various kin relations. Our guest list today is drastically different from what it used to be in the past. There should be no problem with new additions from professional and business connections. But the picture looks quite altered when we discover distant relatives and kinsmen missing, as if distanced by the design of modernity. The contrast is more glaring in case of those who have permanently settled in cities. Gone are the days when a distant cousin visiting the home of in-laws of another was not only welcome but also received the same level of hospitality as would have been extended to the son in law proper. Today distant relatives are literally distanced and increasing distancing among near relatives is a common feature of our social life. The silent bonding and binding that took place under conditions of interdependency is sadly lacking in today's world of market driven ways of life.

Perhaps the younger generation knows better. They are to face the brave new world emerging fast in contemporary times. Faced with the difficulties in adhering to the norms of prohibitions in marriages they are taking recourse to unorthodox solutions transcending boundaries of caste, state and religion generally driven by conscious decision based on personal choice. Several of such cases, where gross violation of rules of exogamy compounded with the violation of the prohibition of marriage in the same village, whether in conformity with or in violation of other norms, have attracted the ire of the community expressed through the traditional *Panchayats* dispensing spot justice. Honour killing has been the normal response in case a member of a lower caste attempts to run away with a Jat girl to marry her. Rural areas are acutely facing the new phenomena of conflict between tradition and individual choice. The city bred cannot imagine the amount of embarrassment to the affected families. Their daily life almost comes to a stand-still. We cannot urbanise rural India in one go. For the present, tradition must prevail but with restraint and innovative approach to find solutions in eases of its violations not in contravention of laws of the land and above all human rights.

21

The Jats in Chachnamah - Some Observations

The Chachnamah is a Persian version of a manuscript in Arabic, containing an account of the conquest of Sindh by Arabs. The original manuscript in Arabic was preserved by one Kazi Ismail of Sakifi family of Alor (Aror) as a family heritage. It was handed over to Ali Kufi for the purpose of presenting the same in Persian language for the benefit of the people at large (the readership in Arabic being negligible in Sindh). The manuscript was a gift very dear to the heart of Ali Kufi as he was already intent on writing an account of the conquest of Hindustan by Muhammad Kasim and the chiefs of Arabia and Syria. Ali Kufi found the original book adorned with jewels of wisdom and embellished with pearls of morality. He prepared a Persian translation of the work in prose (perhaps the original was in Arabic poetry) adorning it with chains of style and ornaments of virtue and religiousness. The creation of Ali Kufi appears to be not merely a literal translation in Persian of the original in Arabic but also a new creation giving a sense of achievement and pride to him as can be seen from his preface to the book. It is not that the original in Arabic contained pure history. According to Ali Kufi apart from an account of the conquest of Hind and Sind (for Sindh to rhyme with Hind)[6] it contained eloquent discourses on religious and state matters and treated of territorial and national peculiarities. There is little doubt that the original in Arabic and its version (with whatever additions) in

6 Elliot and Dowson surmise that the author of *Chachnamah* lived in the eighth or ninth century A.D. and could have relied on the accounts of eyewitnesses (Quoted by Westphal, Sigrid and Heinz in their German work: *Zur Geschichte and Kulture der Jat*, p. 12).

Persian were books of literary merit having at their core the events during the Arab conquest of Sindh.[7]

I do not carry any credentials for speaking on matters of history. But my zeal for understanding the position and role of the Jats as reflected in the Chachnamah have impelled me to commit an audacity. My observations are based on a study of the English translation of the work by Mirza Kalichbegh Fredunbegh, first published from Karachi in 1900 and later reprinted in India in 1979.[8]

One cannot fail to notice the vast amount of material in the Chachnamah having striking similarity with the literary & didactic works, lessons in statecraft and polity contained in ancient Indian compendiums on the respective subjects.[9] In the different discourses by the Wazirs Budhiman and Siyakar that we come across in the Chachnamah appear to be echoes of *Manu Smriti*, Kautilya's *Arthaṣāstra*[10] and pithy sayings of wisdom found in

---

7 At the time of the Arab invasion Sindh included Punjab also and Hind was the name of the territory of North and North-West India, which the Britishers in their earlier contacts called Hindustan.

8 The *Chachnamah, an Ancient History of Sindh*, giving the Hindu period down to the Arab Conquest. Translated from the Persian By Mirza Kalichbeg Fredunbegh, First edition, Karachi, 1900, reprinted in India, 1979.

9 *Chachnamah* refers to books of Hind (p. 23).

10 (i) In the author's description of the love affair between the window of Sahasi Rai and Chach (pp. 16-22) we are reminded of Kautilya's (5.6.41) strategy for keeping a young widow queen from falling for a lover in the kingdom-*Matushchitta-kshobha-bhayatkulyamalpasattvam Chhatram chalakshnayamupanidadhyat.*

(ii) We can also note in the *Chachnamah* (p. 101) the description of the four methods of acquiring a kingdom, which correspond to Kautilya's *Sama* (9.6.21-22), Dana (9.6.23), *Danda* (9.6.53-55) and *Bheda* (9.6.50-51).

(iii) *Chachnamah* prescribes secret tests of wisdom, faith, intelligence and honesty for an envoy sounding so very similar to the four secret tests (the *Upadhas of Dhanna, Artha, Kama and Bhaya*) prescribed by Kautilya (1.10.1-20) to be applied to ministers before their appointment to the post.

various *Subhashitas*[11] come to our mind. As could be gathered from the literal translation in English the Persian version too must have been written in the best tradition of the literary genre. Though Elphinstone may not have agreed if it was suggested to him that the long lectures on matters of statecraft and on questions of propriety introduced in the form of correspondence between Hajjaj and Kasim was only an innovation of the author(s) employed to enhance the level of the work from a mere recounting of the events during the campaigns of the Arabs in Sindh. (Hajjaj's so called correspondence with Kasim and the latter's queries could be compared to the discourse of Shri Krishna to Arjuna imparted on the battleground of Kurukshetra). The distance involved, the flow of events and the logistics involved do not countenance such a correspondence to have actually taken place. But how could a man with literary flavour let such an opportunity go unavailed!

In the narration of the events the bias of the author(s) against the conquered population, especially in the context of the religious agenda is understandable and therefore, due allowance has to be given to that context while sifting facts from fiction. No doubt it is difficult to determine the extent of reliability of the material available in the Chachnamah for the purposes of the history of the times and the people. However, an attempt could be made to cull from the account an idea about the people and their condition at the time of the conquest. It may be worthwhile to notice the references to the Jats and analyse their role before, during and after the Arab conquest of Sindh.

The Jats are described as a major tribe along with the Luhanas living in the region of Brahmanabad in Sindh. The first thing Chach, the son of a priest, did after usurping the throne of Brahmanabad by a stratagem was to curb the Jats and Luhanas, presumably because they must have combined with the Luhanas to oppose him. He took hostages from them to ensure their further non involvement in the conflict and imposed certain restrictions

---

11 Wazir Budhiman's reference (p.45) to five things. which, when they shift from their proper places have a sorry look sounds like an echo of the traditional Indian saying found in the *Subhashitas* : *Sthanabhrashta na shobbante kesha danta nakhakuchanarah.*

on them with a view to disarm them and to prevent them from projecting themselves as belonging to the nobility (p.36-37). He also did not forget to reward those who turned to his side by appointment to high posts.

That Chach had a Jat wife[12] is borne out by the assertion of his son Dahar that there was no impropriety in the latter's marrying his step-sister Bai for the reason that though she was connected with his father, nevertheless she was born of the daughter of the Jats. As if to mitigate his incestuous intent (though only notional) he goes on to pass derogatory remarks against the Jats and describes *Bai* as a woman of foreign origin (good for marriage?). He goes on to refer to a proverb which says "whoever caught hold of a sheep's leg, got milk for himself, and whosoever caught the hand of a Jat, fell down on his face." The Jats are familiar and used to such calumny against them in various periods of history and in absentia even in contemporary times.

We learn about the daring acts of the tribal residents of Debal (including most probably the Jats in detaining and dispossessing some Arab travellers floating to the coast nearby (p. 70). Even Dahar showed his helplessness in curbing these elements when Hajjaj complained to him about the above excesses (pp. 70-71). The Jat agriculturists living around the town of Budhiah formed an important component of the force under the leadership of Kakah Kotak for giving resistance to Kasim. But the credulous leader, going by the soothsayers wilted under pressure and betrayed the Jats, who had rallied to fight but were left leaderless and rudderless - they had neither a leader nor a ruler. The Jats were again in the forefront of the forces of Dahar arrayed on the eastern bank of Indus to stop the cross over by Kasim's troops from the western bank to the territories on the east. It means that the Jats were among the tribes of the plains engaged in agriculture and they could be deployed for military purposes whenever required.

Kasim was aware of the prowess of the Jats. He therefore made all efforts to first win as many of them as possible to his side.

12 If the Luhans were identical with the *Jats Suhandi*, the widow of Sahasi Rai could be Chach's Jat wife, whom he had enticed treacherously.

Divided on the issue as the Jats were, some joined to help the Arabs. There must have been a good number still opposing them. The Jats of the eastern region of Sindh were arrayed in support of Dahar against the Arab forces.

After the occupation of Brahmanabad Kasim asks the surrendering *Wazir* Siyakar as to the treatment meted out to the Jats by Chach and his son Dahar since he himself would like to continue the same arrangement. Siyakar lists the restrictions and obligations earlier placed on the Jats, which Kasim decides to be continued It may be noted that the Jats are described here to belong to the Luhana tribe. The other two tribes Lakhas and Sammas are also described as Luhanas. It can be deduced from the above that Jats were among the three prominent tribes of Sindh and were sometimes taken as identical with Luhanas and at others as separate from them. The lists of restrictions and obligations imposed on the Jats on both the occasions were more or less identical. The salient points of these restrictions were disarming of the Jats, a dress code indicating their identity and moving out barefoot and bare head. Among the obligations were serving as guides for travellers, rendering of services like supply of firewood to the royal kitchen and helping the injured in cases of accidents in their vicinity. But the words coming out of the mouth of Kasim about Jats indicate an utter contempt which he had in his mind for them verily for the reason of their standing in opposition to him. However, may be inadvertently, Kasim does not fail to mention that there was no distinction of high or low among the Jats. It is true to-day. Kasim also imposed a punitive tribute to suppress the Jats as they were perceived as potential rebels at any time as their spirit had been undaunted. A number of those who fought against him were made prisoners of war and were dispatched to Hajjaj, the Persian governor of Iraq as part of the war booty. This event is corroborated by Biladhuri who according to H.M. Eliot has stated that Hajjaj received from Kasim not only gold and other material wealth but also prisoners of war with their families and livestock.[13] German sociologist couple in a monograph, published in 1964

13 H.M. Elliot, edited by J. Dowson, *The History of India*, *The Muhammadan Period*, Calcutta, 1955, pp. 59, 62, 64, 65, 75.

have traced these migrants as the ancestors of the modern Madan tribe living as buffalo breeders in the Marshy lands of southern Iraq.[14] They have also plotted the possible alternative routes taken for the movement along with their cattle (buffaloes) towards Iraq. The Jats or *Jaats* of Sindh (including modem Sindh and both East and West Punjab) continued to pursue their vocation of agriculture and cattle rearing for centuries. Those of the west came under the influence of Islam while those of the east remained in the Hindu fold. Many of the latter branched off and became the bedrock of Sikhism. But they are proud of their Jat identity irrespective of the persuasion of different religions. But they are proud of their Jat identity irrespective of the persuasion of different religions. It is relevant to note here that the author of *Mujmal Tawarikh* (early 12th century A.D.) making use of a Persian version of an Arabic translation of a Indian book, *Manjushrimulakalpa* states on the one hand that the Jats (*Zutt*) were one of the two tribes (Jats and Meds) of Sindh, and that this country was the "country of the *Zutt*", while on the other he remarks that "By the Arabs the Hindus are called Jats" and further states that ultimate peace was brought about by settling some *Brahmanas* in their midst.[15] In the *Chachnamah* also we read the suppression of the Jats by the *Brahmana* rulers Chacha and Dahar. Centuries passed, regimes changed, religions changed, but the Jats remained the same or got worse. Whatever is history or whatever is myth in *Chachnamah*, it is hardly material. If Jat is the term used for the farmer or the cattle breeder he has been at the receiving end as far as privileges or positions are concerned.

---

14 Westphal, Dr. Sigrid and Dr. Heinz : *The Jat of Pakistan*, Berlin, 1964; reprinted in Pakistan.

15 Westphal, Sigrid and Heinz, *Zur Geschichte Und Kultur der Jat*, p. 12.

22

Hookah Hook

Fully aware of the scientific findings regarding the ill effects of use of tobacco products on the health of the people a Central Health Minister, Dr. Ramo Dasa had been leading a relentless campaign against the use of the substance. His almost obsessive concern on the issue had left no holds barred for him. He did not hesitate to first issue personal appeals to celebrities to desist from smoking publicly and then went ahead in getting a suitable legislation prohibiting the representation of smoking on screen enacted. His belief that the screen hero being a role model for the young minds could greatly influence them to take to smoking. The cigarette smoking popular cinema icon Shahrukh Khan did favourably respond to the appeal issued to men of his profession. This perhaps was a fond belief as the Apex Court recently ruled while rejecting the provision of such a flimsy (filmy?) nature. Though the court took its stand on the principle of freedom of artistic representation the ban looked unnecessary as such. We are aware that the cinema audience has matured a good deal as has the cinema itself over the years. Our young men (or women) are no more enamoured of the hero or the villain releasing chains of rings of smoke while smoking a cigarette.

But the indefatigable minister having both the moralists and the health providers on his side, the powerful tobacco lobby notwithstanding, had indeed moved resolutely in slapping a ban on smoking in public places (defined quite comprehensively) through law. It is every body's hope that the measure will go a long way in hooking a good number of people, especially the young people off the fag and give the desired relief to unwilling passive smokers thronging public places like buses and railways (discipline in air is already in place) and even parks. But an omnibus fiat of law like the one we have in place now, either continues to remain oblivious or willingly overlooks a large section of our population, mainly rural, given to institutionalized smoking. How this ban like many other similar ones is going to work in rural areas, not only for the reason of mere logistics of enforcement but also (and mainly) for the reason of more deeper and cultural issues involved in the matter is any body's guess.

An observer of the rural ways would bear it out that people in villages generally have a differentiated attitude towards individual smoking and community smoking. The underlying reason for this differentiation could be the cigarette (or *bidi*) being perceived as an intruding individualistic smoking medium in an established traditional *Hookah* culture of the village communities integrated into the totality of their social code.

We may here like to muse over how *Hookah* hooks people into camaraderie of its own kind well linked with the kinship relations in its working. Though with the onset of modernity, leading to dismantling of the joint family system and the ever-increasing hectic life style, the *hookah* culture has lost some of its past glow (or glory in several connotations!), yet it continues to serve as the focal point for social networking and seeking shared relaxation. *Hookah* continues to be one of the parameters of the expression of social beliefs and practices well ingrained in the life of rural communities since ages, it has served as a measure of some sort of time keeping, generally indicating small breaks in the course of working or waiting. It was to underscore this place of importance accorded to *hookah* in the sedentary life style of the village folk till fifty years ago that on the occasion of fairs, a special day was set apart for holding *Hookah* Fair. Potters from far and wide participated in this unique fair offering their earthen *hookahs* of various designs and sizes for sale at reasonable rates. The village folk fully utilized this opportunity and made purchases of stocks enough to last till the time of the next fair. Those interested in acquiring metal *Hookahs* (*pharsi*<*parsi*<Persian) of a more fancy design, however, had to visit the market in the town or the city.

Hookah was no mere contraption for smoking tobacco. It represented a culture and served as a symbol of communal bonding and close fraternity enveloping the *gotra* and caste aspects in its operation. It was shared among the members of the community of equals and offered as a means of hospitality to a visitor. Before joining a smoking party a stranger would invariably ascertain the communal/caste identity of the group. Denial of the privilege of sharing a *hookah* was among the major measures of social sanctions imposed against a person as punishment for violating a social code. On occasions *Hookah* also served as a swear object as did the all-important cattle like cow or bullock (in contrast of the buffalo). The material, size and design of the *hookah* indicated the standing of the owner in his community. The higher the gathering in a smoking parlour the higher the popularity it indicated in respect of the owner. At such places the *hookah* could be noticed flaunting a *Rakhi* on *Rakshabandhan* day, signifying its instrumentality in promoting bond of brotherhood. Some owners would not forget to mount their *hookah* on a free wheeled disc attached to a sturdy plate for easy rotations. Proper up keep of the *hookah* was no less important. The aroma would wane out unless the *hookah* was intermittently overhauled by replacing the stale water with fresh one and the waste deposits removed from the interiors of its various tubes with the help of a pull through *(gaj)*. A fine and smooth gurgling sound when put into operation was indicative of the desired level of performance of the contraption.

The *brahmanas* practiced exclusivity in not sharing their *hookahs* with people of other castes. However, the Jats and other middle level castes shared their *hookahs* among themselves, leaving the members of the *dalit* castes outside their circle. Out in the crop fields the farmers carried their personal mini *hookahs* called *huktis*. *A* midi *hookah* used by a smaller group or an individual was called *kalai* (perhaps for its pot being made of nickel plated metal). *Narial* would be the name of a still smaller *hukti* if the pot was made of coconut shell (and by extension of meaning any small *(hukti of such shape)* Farmers working in close proximity in the fields relaxed the caste restrictions in sharing the *hukti*. However, the relaxation in case of the members of the *harijan* community was limited only to the sharing of the earthen top fire-pot *(chillum)*. Tobacco under a round lid (*thekari)* was placed atop an earthen ball trapped on the hole in the middle of the fire pot fixed on the smaller stump of the *hookah.* Continued supply of tobacco and fire tinder, were the main ingredients for keeping the smoking sessions go on and on. Tobacco supply was hardly a problem as most of the participants kept their own stock of locally grown home-made tobacco in small pouches (*kothalis)* safely tucked in the pleats of their waist band (*adband<ardhabandha)* of their *dhoti* and generally every one present would volunteer to offer at least a measure (*pat)* to escape the sobriquet of a *patpad.* In the comity of smokers one could find connoisseurs of different grades of tobacco Viz. weak, strong and medium, majority preferring the last named. Fire tinder could be obtained from the reserved stock kept ready simmering in an ash covered fire pit called *poor* (hearth) in one corner of a parlour. The tinder was replenished by an additional supply of pieces of cow dung cakes buried in the ash pit arranged in a queue, one touching another ahead. In case of emergency the fire places of the households in the same street were sought after but not before discreet enquiry made from the concerned housewife was answered in the affirmative. When all other sources of fire tinder were exhausted the rich stock invariably intact under the simmering earthen milk pots *(kadhawanis)* of households would be accessed. Sometimes an enterprising young man would not forget to help himself by laying hand on the pot for a lump of creamy crust as a bonus. But such forays were limited to very friendly households. As a general norm cross street attempts to get fire tinder were not countenanced. It was, however, pass if a youngster ventured out on such a mission. Showing deference to the privacy of the women folk of the street was the main consideration behind such self-imposed restrictions.

The first few pulls at the recharged *hookah,* following the customary inaugural one by the senior most among those present were to be made by a junior member of the smoking party (determined on the basis of hierarchy of age and *gotra)* till the tobacco got ignited (*sulgana*) especially if the instrument had been lying idle for quite some time. He also had the responsibility to manipulate the instrument holding it from the calf region *(gatta pakarna)* and offer it to the other members gathered turn-by-turn starting with the senior most among those present. If per chance the protocol (again determined on the basis of seniority of degree in clan relationship and age) of the persons concerned turned out to be at par, each one would push the mouthpiece (*nay)* of the *hookah* forward to the next man in the manner of passing a buck. Similar was the norm when the group engaged in smoking comprised only a father-in-law and a son-in-law. Here the seniority in age of the father- in-law came into clash with the kin wise higher degree of a son-in-law as a bride taker, hence the middle path.

23

Name, Surname and Nickname: Identity Issues

When Shakespeare declared 'what is in a name ! a rose is a rose by any other name' he was not minimising the importance of name but was underlining the intrinsic value of things. The Indian version of the saying paradox in terms-*aankh ke andhe naam nayansukh* underscores the need to name things and persons not in contradiction of the qualities they happen to carry. A name according to our tradition reflects any of the four elements, namely category, quality, matter and functionality. We may recall how the creator god Prajapati, when himself born first as a child, pressed forward the need for getting a name for himself and how he felt satisfied only after receiving as many as eight names- all expressing various functions attributed to him and a ninth one i.e. Kumara for his young appearance of a babe as bonus so to say. It is a different matter that the *Puranas* later transferred all these names to Shiva, the last (Kumara), going to one of his sons Skanda-Karttikeya, the famous Subrahmanya or Murugan of the Tamil Tract. Richness and multiplicity has marked the names of our gods and goddesses. Who has not heard of the thousand names of Vishnu (*Vishnu-sahasranama)* and the efficacy their remembrance brings to the devotees?

Coming to the mundane plain we find our socio-religious books commending how we should be going about giving names to our new born. The *Ashvalayana Grihyasutra*, as also the *Paraskara Grihyasutra* recommend that on the tenth day of the birth a child should be given a name comprising two or four syllables, in case of a male and three or five, in case of a female, thus maintaining the number even and odd respectively. Further both insisted that the syllables contained only sonant letters *ga, gha, da, dha* etc. and that a semi vowel *ya* or *va* be at the end if required. Another aspect of personal name was that it should carry primary suffix *(krit)* at the end rather than a secondary (*taddhita*) one and also that it should be one compound word, though having several component words.

Apart from linguistic moorings names reflect the religious and social beliefs and influences. Thus names also carry an imprint of the social, personal predilections and cultural identity of a person. A person's name is the most frequently used term in his/her life and thereby the most likeable one. Since personal names from the very ancient times have tended to be constituted of more than one part put into one compounded form it was natural that names continued to be meaningful and it may be interesting to note the nature and range of the different components. *Vishva* continues to be a component of names right from the vedic age (Vishwamitra) to the modern days (*Vishwa Mohan*). Similar is the journey of the second component *Sena* as seen in *Vishwasena, Nagasen, Harisena and Mitrasena* crossing millenniums. Let us not miss to note that the component *sena* is the remnant of the term *sena* (army).

The practice of abridging names can be traced to hoary past. Pāṇini, the celebrated Sanskrit grammarian noted such tendency and provided a rule for the same. For economy (or need) of effort the second member of a compound name like *Vyaghra-Ajina* or *Deva-Datta* could be dropped in order to obtain the desired number of vowels (between two to four or five) as mentioned above. However, in part compensation, *ka*, *iya or ila* could be added to the abridged name. For example *Deva-Datta* would be turned into *Devaka, Deviya or Devila.* Generally such a course was adopted when expressing love especially for the young children. This could be said to be the precursor of the modern day practice of having pet names like Bittoo, Vicky, Pappu etc. This shortening of names was a common practice in all cases till the not so remote past. We had *Harke* for *Hari Krishna. Rama* for *Rama Chandra, Ome* for *Om Prakash* and so on.

The elements of nature like the sun, the moon, the air and the earth along with their various synonyms have richly contributed to the corpus of names used throughout India. Similar is the case of gods and their spouses. The most common pattern where gods figure in personal names is the one which has the second component as *Datt (Datta* to be precise). Here the belief that children are god given gift appears to be working at the back of the minds of parents. It is more true in cases where earlier there had been infant deaths in the family.

The practice of persons being named and known as the scions of their father starting form very early times continues to this day. The Sanskrit grammarian fixes accent on the first syllable of the father's name followed by the second part of the name as in *Damaka-putra.* It underlines the importance of someone being the son of a man named Damaka. We find this happening in almost all cases of stating the identity of a person whether present or in absentia. Perhaps this has something to do with the law (in its old form) of inheritance tilting in favour of the male. In Maharashtra and in most cases in Gujarat the name of a person contains the name of his father as the second component. The *gotra* system also works in the domain of the male. A female gets her *gotra* from her male ancestor till she marries. After marriage she gets the *gotra* name of her husband. There is a wide spread misconception about this feature being a sign of male chauvinism. This in fact again has something to do with share in property and succession, issues. When a woman after marriage dons the *gotra* name of her husband it indicates the merger of her identity with that of her husband. And that is the meaning, given to marriage by all cultures. Some time back cine star Sanjay Dutt, in the context of his being heir to the *gotra* of his father, made an innocent and matter of fact advisory remark about the propriety of her sister Priya (who retains her father's *gotra* even after her marriage),-adopting her husband's *gotra* name only to invite sharp reaction, not only from Priya herself but several others, including some women groups. Mercifully the spat involving the two siblings did not last long. Perhaps there was equal merit in the arguments advanced by the two opposing sides. We know of Prabhavati Gupta, the daughter of Chandragupta-II retaining her father's *gotra* name viz. *Dharana* even after her joining the Vakataka family through marriage. Today there is no dearth of women adopting the name of their marital family without dropping the *gotra* name of their father. But interestingly this double surname/*gotra* name is not seen to be percolating to the next generation for the simple logic of proliferation into unmanageable proportions.

But a child whose father's name could not be ascertained would be known by the name of his mother, though not without inviting derogatory frowns front society. In colloquial parlance such a child is known as *gellad* (the illegitimate one), notwithstanding some modern day safeguards given by law. But the case of a child identified from among many siblings from several mothers married in a polygamous system (in the past) by the name of his/her mother falls in an altogether different category. We have several such Satavahana princes of the second century A.D. But interestingly the identity of a child (or adult for that matter) at his/ her mothers parents' home is determined by her maiden name, there being no issues of inheritance involved and there being no percolation of the identity of the child's father in the community there except as a bride taker.

Then we have a wide gamut of nicknames current at the informal plain of communication. Nicknames arise due to several factors operating in the life of persons and include both positive and derogatory. The positive ones have their origin in some good deed (*sadhu),* appearance (*suthra*, *mota, patla*), colour of the skin *(bhura),* height *(lamba, chhota) etc.* Some nicknames, which are derogatory, can be attributed to the associating of certain physical deformities, deficiencies or habits (real or imagined) with their subjects. For example we have *kana* (one eyed), *ganja* (bald), *langda* (lame) *toonda* (stump handed), *landa* (with small tail), *surda* (untidy) (*boda)* having broken teeth) etc. In both the categories they initially get currency for quick determination of identity. But when they get passed on to be applied to the members of the next generations they are taken as *byonk* of the family and in most cases to the members of the extended family taking a plural form. We have the famous story how a family struggling to shed off their *byonk, surde* of several generations spent a fortune in organizing a lavish community feast with the request and hope that the family would no more be called by the *byonk* only to hear to their amazement and dismay the rich tributes laced with a rich dose of the *byonk, surde* for their demonstration of community feeling.

Again there are good number of cases where, qualification (Shastri), title (Rai), post (Kulpati), profession (Vakil). Vocation (Purohit) etc turn into *byonk* for the succeeding generations. However, in case of the *byonk* being quite pleasing and flattering, it did not take long for it to graduate to the degree of *gotra* and ultimately supersede the same. Using *gotra* as a surname is a common practice in modem times but the ancient practice of using Sharma for Brahmanas, Verma for Kshatriyas and Gupta for Vaishyas (of the later date) can be noticed as an equally preferred option at all times.

Names of strong and well-built animals have been contributing a member of the personal names over a long period. Thus we have had names like *Naravyaghra*, *Nararshabha* to be the favourite as a component of names dislodging many a time-honoured and popular components. Its popularity was so remarkable that it came to be added as the third and last component if either of the prevailing two components was (indispensable. *Singh* appearing as the second and final component in most names became the norm in Punjab. Rajasthan and Haryana during the Mughal period. In case of the adherents of Sikh religion it formed an integral and compulsory part of names mostly coming at the end. It traveled to Uttar Pradesh as the third component without dislodging the time honoured conventional components. In most parts of the country all those who prefer to identify themselves as *kshatriya* groups, invariably add this component to their names. Hitherto vast sections of *dalits* in the north and the north-west see this as a means of demonstrating their awareness about social equality. Thus we notice *Simha* replacing *Das* as a part of the process of social engineering currently happening at a fast pace. The already upwardly mobile sections of the *dalit* population have demonstrated their penchant for going for sanskritised and buddhistic names. A kind of social churning in search of identity is on and we hope to see many a gem coming out as a result.

24

A Backward View on a Forward Issue: Reservation for Women in Legislatures

News reports have it that the new government would like to pass the bill providing for representation for women in legislatures. It is umpteen number of years since the issue was mooted to be introduced as a bill in and passed by the two Houses of our Parliament. Notwithstanding the declared majority support to the measure, an appropriate bill was withdrawn at the introduction stage with an intriguing alacrity at the slightest show of opposition from isolated quarters. The Bill attracted similar response from the different regimes in government. Willy nilly it got introduced during the year 2013 only to be put on the back burner awaiting an elusive consensus. But the pity is that hardly any national level debate has been provoked on the issue except the elite fora where, sadly enough, the debates remained confined to unilateral candour. Neither those who held the opposite view did spell out their reservations in a constructive manner. Even among the members of the ruling party at different times, reservations continued to linger with regard to the wisdom of the measure. This could be easily gauged from the body language of good number of members on either side of the divide on each occasion the Bill was stalled and withdrawn at the introductory stage. It appeared to the cynic that those who were opposing the bill were in fact obliging those who sponsored it.

Mercifully, the bill was at last introduced in the Upper house some time back, perhaps to keep it alive on technical grounds for a little longer period. The alibi of reaching a national consensus came handy for the procrastination witnessed impatiently by those who had wanted to hustle through. Nothing can be said with certainty about the fate of the bill. It is yet to be introduced in the lower house. Already there are signals for negotiating the percentage of reservations for women from those who were vehemently opposed to the concept in its present form for quite some time (in the manner of 'something is better than nothing'). Or, have they already seen the writing on the wall. So perhaps, a cult is coming on the strength of its emotional appeal and it is almost blasphemy to talk against it or to even point out the perils befalling the social fabric of our country, which still continues to be a rural entity in spite of the outwardly urbanised chunks growing out of emaciated rural population.

The ostensible purpose of reserving seats in legislatures is to accede to the better half her due share in a bid to empower her to serve as an engine of progress for the females of our country. On the face of it, it is a pious wish and nobody should have reason to fight with it. It is however, not understood how the presence of a greater number of women in any legislative body would make any difference in making laws to improve the lot of women. In modern times we have witnessed with pride the concerns expressed and legislation passed ensuring the improvement of the lot of women by legislators among whom there had been a negligible number of the fair sex. And let it be made clear that it was no charity doled out to women by men. Men were, indeed, legislating either in favour of a mother or a wife or a sister or a daughter. The paradigm of 'man-woman' as two wheels of the same cart, ensuring a smooth ride on life's journey is as transcendental as one would think in the fast changing times of the automobile world. One would therefore, like to go into the dynamics of the issue through a backward view.

When our constitution makers (quite an enlightened lot!) provided for reservations for the various depressed communities they were not unaware of the still degraded position of women among these sections of our society. It was not an oversight on their part, one can say, not to talk of women separately in that context. Surely our wise men (and women) of today are entitled to talk about the need to give reservation and through it empowerment to the most depressed among the community of women. The history of the growth and development of the political class in post-independence India compels us to take note of trends which do not strongly demonstrate our concerns for strengthening of the democratic model. The coalescing of the political, intellectual and ruling classes is taking place at such a fast pace and not always unbrazenly that the masses find it difficult (or many a time impossible!) to keep pace with them to reap the fruits of 'self rule'. In a scheme of things where at least 30% (or a brokered 20 %) of the legislators are women the party managers (of any dispensation) would find it more convenient to have things their way. But from where this number would be drawn is any body's guess. One can assume that the classes would have it and the masses would be left out of the race here too. The implication is that the number of new arrivals among the backward legislators would be reduced. To put it differently the number of legislators from backward classes will go down drastically.

The myth of reservation on the basis of sex serving as a catalytic for the improvement of the lot of woman in general can be seen to be breaking in the regime of *Panchayats* and Municipalities. It is no secret that by and large women representatives serve as proxies of their male patrons in the family (father or brother). Let us imagine there would be educated and smart women (of whom there is no dearth, we admit) in legislatures taking up women's causes and fighting for them. The question is who will work for society, as by corollary, men should be working for the cause of men. Society is not male or female specific. Therefore, fragmenting representation on the basis of sex would not serve the best interest of society. It would amount to vertical division of the man-woman solid pillar of our social structure. It is not to deny that women in our country do not have enough space of their own which could ensure safety; security and desired freedom. It is also true that our laws covering social, economic and personal life, in spite of great amount of reform, still need to be made more woman friendly and enforceable. But our starting at the top in giving reservation to women in legislatures, when a good amount of work awaits our attention to be taken up immediately without courting avoidable controversy, betrays our concern for the form rather than the substance. One railway minister has demonstrated how a small step of setting apart 'women only' coaches in the local trains can serve as a means, both for giving confidence to the hapless female passengers and serve as a signal to those who would like to innovate to create a woman friendly environment in their respective charge. Already schemes are in place for the amelioration of the condition of woman in need. These need to be multiplied and strengthened. We have witnessed how a small measure of reserving some seats for women in the Delhi Metro trains has added to the comfort of female passengers who now throng the facility in large numbers mostly unescorted. It may be necessary to resort to such exclusive steps to begin with but our ultimate aim should be to create an environment where a woman does not feel handicapped simply because of her gender. In the developed countries efforts have been made to create separate safe enclaves in public places like Parks; transport system and even hotels in cities like Tokyo, New York and Moscow. The ancient law giver Manu had advocated safety and security to women at all stages of her life. It is, however, a pity that his prescription in the following piece has gone totally misconstrued in popular perception: *pita rakshati kaumare, bharta rakshati yauvane| varddhakye putrah rakshanti, na stri svatantryamarhati||* [The father is responsible for the safety and security of the female till her marriage, after which the husband takes over that responsibility, and the children take care of her in old age. A woman, indeed, should never be left to fend for herself (uncared for).There should be no doubt left about his stand vis-a-vis women in his observation: *yatra naryastu pujyante ramante tatra devatah* i.e. gods would love to live in a society where women have a place of honour and respect.

Imagine the possible scenario if the reservation regime proposed now falls into place. We are already miffed by the nexus of various interest groups in our democratic polity. The most powerful being the steel frame of bureaucrats, who await the chance of their spouses arriving to directly bat for them in the legislatures (it is not difficult to guess what class would reap the first fruits of the reservation regime), making their power claws more lethal, not a healthy development for democracy. Elitism has already marked the hue of our legislatures. No one would fail to notice, how through the capture of political parties kins have combined to corner seats. There are a large number of mixed doubles in our Parliament either in the same house or in the two houses combined. These father-son/daughter combinations are going to multiply as and when seats are reserved for women. The customary argument 'the people want them' is certainly going to be the ready-made response of all those who would be responsible to explain the phenomenon. The common man (also woman!) would be left wondering at the denouement of the charade of a very popular saga of women's empowerment. Or are we entitled to imagine, in a lighter vein though, that our legislatures would have a redeeming feature, as in the presence of women in a substantial number we would have our speakers not to have to stretch substantially to control members, aggressive both in language and manners. Also, one can trust the sartorial spectrum in the lower houses taking a right (if not a U) turn, though we may not witness many turncoats. In the end one should hope that the houses (or at least the lobbies!) would not give a deserted look during session times. And shall we not hope that repartee, a rare commodity these days, would grow in abundance being home (house!) grown as it were.

Appendix-1

Some Jat Gotras:

	Present Jat Gotra	Sanskrit Equivalent	Derived from	Possible Original
1	Aujalan	Aujjwalāyana	Aujjwala	Ujjwala
2.	Kadyan	Kātyāyana	Kātya	Kata
3.	Kanjlan	Kānjalāyana	Kānjala	Kanjala
4.	Chandarayan	Chāndrāyana	Chāndra	Chandra
5.	Thakran	Thākrāyana	Thākara	Thakura
6.	Dehlan	Daihalāyana	Daihala	Dehala
7.	Baaswan	Bāswāyana	Bāsava	Basu
8.	Johalan	Jauhalāyana	Jauhala	Juhala
9.	Shaaklan	Shākalyāyana	Shākalya	Shakala
10.	Aulakh	Aulikara		
11.	Khokar	Kharaparika		
12.	Kaak	Kāka		
13.	Gujar	Gurajara		
14.	Chedi	Chedi		
15.	Chalukya	Chaluky		
16.	Pawar	Paramāra		
17.	Wahik	Wālhika		
18.	Yodhey	Yaudheya		
19.	Rathi	Rāshtrika		
20.	Solanki	Chālukya		

21.Sagwan Shākavān

22.Sheokhand Shivaskanda

23.Joon Prārjuna

(The names of the gotras have invariably Sanskrit suffixes at the end such as Vat, mat, iyas, ka, Ii etc. indicating Sanskritic/vedic propensities of the Jāts.)

Appendix-2

Terms for Relationships:

[Jāts have been living in an integrated social system of relationships so characteristic of the early Aryan tribal society. The members of the extended family (and ultimately all members of the tribe) were mutually related to each other in a well defined relationship. These relationships come into reckoning in the clan (gotra) system of brother-hood which cements a caste]

Modern Form	**Sanskrit**	**English**
Maata	Mātri	Mother
Amma	Ambā	Mummy
Pita/ Baabu	Pitri	Father
Poot /Dhih	Putra/Putri/Duhitā	Son/Daughter
Beta/Beti	Vatsa/Vatsā	Dear Son/Daughter
Potaa/ Poti	Pautra/ Pautri	Grand-Son/ Daughter
Daadaa/ Daadi	Pitāmaha/Pitāmahi	Father's Father / Mother
Naana/Naani	Nānri/Nānri	Mother's Father/Mother
Dohta/Dohti	Dauhitra/ Dauhitri	Daughter's Son/Daughter
Bhaai/Bahin	Bhrātri /Bhagini	Brother/ Sister
Bhanoi	Bhagini-odha	Sister's Husband
Saala/li	Shyālaka/likā	Wife's Brother /Sister
Taaoo	Pitrivya	Father's elder Brother
Kaaka	Kāniyaska	father's younger brother
Bhabi	Bhratrijāyā/Bhāryā	Brother's wife
Devar	Devara	Husband's younger brother
Jyeth	Jyeshtha	Husband's elder brother
Sasur	Shvasura	Father-in- law

Saasu	Shvashru	Mother-in-law
Tayasara	Pitrivyashvasura	Father-in-law's elder brother
Pitasara	Pitrivyashvasura	Father-in-law's younger brother
Maamaa	Mātula	Mother's brother
Maami	Mātulāni	Mother's brother's wife
Molasara	Mātula Shvasura	Husband's mother's Brother
Buaa	Pitribyā	Father's Sister
Phoophad	Pitribyodhā	Father's Sister's Husband
Mausi/ Mausa	Mātrisvasri/	Mother's Sister/ Her Husband
Bhatijaa/Bhatiji	Bhrātrija/Bharatrijā	Brother's Son/ Daughter
Bhanjaa	Bhaginija	Sister's Son
Bhaanji	Bhaginijā	Sister's Daughter
Nanad	Nanandri	Husband's Sister
Nanadoyiya	Nanandodhā	Sister's Husband
Pihar	Pitrighara	Father's Home
Saasra	Shvasurālaya	Father-in-law's Home

Appendix-3

Flora and Fauna:

Present Form	**Sanskrit**	**English**
Gau	Gau	Cow
Bulad	Balivarda	Bullock
Mhains/Bhains	Mahishi	Buffalo
Bachhda	Vatsatara	Calf
Ghodaa	Ghotaka	Horse
Gadhaa	Gardbha	Donkey
Oont	Ushtra	Camel
Kuttaa	Kukkura	Dog
Hiran	Harina	Deer
Sih	Simha	Lion
Sussa	Shashaka	Hare
Ulloo	Ulooka	Owl
Soor	Sookara	Pig
Billi	Vidaali	Cat
Moosaa	Mooshaka	Rat
Mor	Mayoora	Peacock
Kabootara	Kapota	Pigeon
Shuggaa	Shuka	Parrot
Saanp	Sarpa	Snake
Bichhoo	Vrishchika	Scorpion
Chidiya	Chatakā	Sparrow
Kachhuaa	Kachhapa	Tortoise

Giddha	Gridhra	Eagle
Nyola	Nakuala	Mangoose
Seh	Srimara	Porcupine
Siyar	Shrigāla	Jackal
Gehoon	Godhooma	Wheat
Chanaa	Chanaka	Gram
Iikh	Ikshu	Sugarcane
Kapaas	Kaarpaasa	Cotton
Daabha	Darbha	Sharp-edged Grass
Doob	Doorvaa	Grass
Kair	Karira	Shrub
Neem	Nimba	Margosa tree
Saamaka	Shyamāka	A Type of Grass
Maash	Maasha	Black Pulse
Patta	Patram	Leaf
Mooli	Moolaka	Reddish
Bel	Valli	Creeper
Mitti	Mrittika	Mud
Âmra	Aam	Mango
Beri	Badari	Plum Tree
Phool	Puppha Pushpa	Flower
Kela	Kadali	Banana

Appendix-4

Food and Drinks

Present Form	**Sanskrit**	**English**
Ghee	Ghrita	Clarified Butter
Pāni	Pāniya	Water
Doodha	Dugdha	Milk
Dahi	Dadhi	Curd
Shakkar	Sharkarā	Sugar(raw)
Gud	Guda	Jaggery
Shila	Sheetala	Cold
Taatta	Tapta	Hot
Kadwa	Katu	Sour
Meetha	Mishtha	Sweet
Noon/loon	Lavana	Salt
Haldi	Haridrā	Turmeric
Saag	Shaka	Vegetable
Kheer	Kshira	Rice-Milk Pudding

Appendix-5

Dress and Ornaments

Present Form	**Sanskrit**	**English**
Angarkhaa	Angarakshaka	Gown
Pahnaavaa	Paridhāna	Clothes
Angiyaa	Angikā	Bodice
Chogaa	Kanchuka	Gown
Kangan	Kankana	Bracelet
Kanthi	Kanthikaa	Necklace
Kanphool	Karnapoora	Ear Hanging
Nath	Nathini	Nose Ring
Newari	Nupura	Anklet
Angoothi	Angulikā	Ring
Kadulla	Kata	Bracelet
Boojni	Vajini	Ear hanging
Galasri	Galashri	Necklace
Jhaalra	Jhallara	Garland

"A meridian through the town of Sirhind or Sirhand (head of Hind), nearly due north of Patiala ...... roughly divided the Punjab proper from Hindustan and the Punjabi language from the Hindi language, and forms the eastern boundary of the Sikh religion". (Ibbetson)